AnnaBelle's Spirit

Dreams In The Mist

Carolyn Sue Morris

authorHOUSE®

AuthorHouse™
1663 Liberty Drive
Bloomington, IN 47403
www.authorhouse.com
Phone: 1-800-839-8640

First published by AuthorHouse 9/3/2009

ISBN: 978-1-4490-1401-8 (e)
ISBN: 978-1-4490-1399-8 (sc)
ISBN: 978-1-4490-1400-1 (hc)

Library of Congress Control Number: 2009908499

Printed in the United States of America
Bloomington, Indiana

This book is printed on acid-free paper.

Contents

AnnaBelle   1947

For
My Mother
AnnaBelle "Wicker" Bollan
February 25, 1927 to October 4, 2007

As before, I wouldn't have had the inspiration without you in my life. I feel your presence each and every day. I feel your hand, as well as my own, in the writing of these books. I feel your love surrounding me. I feel you are still a phone call away.

Until I see you again.......
I love you.
Your Daughter,
Carolyn Sue

Preface

AnnaBelle's spirit never leaves me, she stays close in my realm of reality. She's the flash of light, the shadow passing quickly, the breath of air on my cheek. She's comfort when my heart aches, she's a burst of energy when I tire.

A world of dreams, a lifetime of journeys. Together we fought the odds, separately we fought our battles. The ending......always the same.

I close my eyes and see the dreams now past. I cannot bring them back, though some, I desperately wish I could.

AnnaBelle lived with the choices she made in her lifetime, as I now live with mine. Some we alone controlled, some controlled by others. Yet in the end I clearly see, the powers that control the ages will somehow take care of the past, present, and future.

So let the love begin in your heart, as it should. Allow the ones that haunt your dreams to enter your heart, as they should. Keep your secrets deep inside where they are safe, as you should. For in the end that's what you will have, the love, the dreams and the secrets. These will live forever in your heart, along with AnnaBelle's spirit, as they should.

Prologue

"AnnaBelle's Spirit" is a follow-up to my first published work, "The Journey, The Dreams, & AnnaBelle". In hind site, this is the book that should have been written first. With this writing I have tried to give the story more depth without being repetitive. I did not include any of my poetry in this book, except one I had written to Mom during the plane ride home after her passing.

The story of AnnaBelle is a tribute to the life of my mother, and the spirit that constantly drove her life. Born in Kentucky, she carried the memories of the hills, and her youth spent there with pride and dignity. She was one of the most beautiful and fascinating women I have ever known. Life with her was anything but average or mundane. Because of AnnaBelle's choices, my journey has been more of an adventure than some people will experience. Because of my own choices, that same journey has taken my heart in many directions. I live with the spirits of those that I have loved, and I live with their memories etched in my heart. But most importantly, I live with their faces forever in my dreams. As you can see, I believe in the power of spirits, not only the spirit that drives us through life, but the spirit we become after life. I know I am surrounded by the spirits of those I love. Some stronger than others, but they are all here.

AnnaBelle's journey from Kentucky to Indiana was her first. There were many places, people, and events that would rule her life. Her memories are her own, and some will remain so. I thank God I took the time to listen, she shared so many thoughts and dreams with me. The dates, times, and facts included in this book are directly from Mom. Her life was full of surprises, from the marriage she had dreamed of, to the nightmare it became.

I love AnnaBelle for the adventures we shared, for the endless moving, for the many people we met along the way, and for never a dull moment. Most of all, I love her for being my Mother. She always told me that she had two things in life that no one could ever take away from her, those two things were her daughters. As the youngest, I have always known she is the one constant in my life, and that she will never be completely taken away from me. Though God took her presence, he has left the memory of her life, her love, and her wonderful spirit forever in my heart. She stays there, with the others; they control my thoughts and dreams. There, they will live forever.

Acknowledgments

I have to thank Mom for sharing her many memories with me. I will forever hold dear our endless conversations, for being there when I needed her, for always loving me, and most of all, for being my Mother.

I hold a special place in my heart for Uncle Bud & Aunt Darlene. I have to thank them not only for their help and support with my writing, and sharing their memories with me, but for continuing to be there for me when I have needed someone to talk to. Their love for Mom carries over to me. I am blessed to have them in my life.

John continues to be patient with me. For what reason, I do not know. But I do appreciate his support, and the fact that he doesn't read my work. He say's he wouldn't like it. I believe he is being brutally honest, but in the end, we are both better off with his choices.

The support and help I have received from my children, grandchildren, and sister, has been phenomenal. With their help in promoting my first book, they have helped make this second work possible. Their faith in me is amazing.

As I've said before, I have incredible friends. They, too, have supported my efforts in writing. Those that have read my work say they like it, and want to read more. We'll see, little did they know this was coming. I love them all. I'm reminded of an old saying, "Tell me quick before I faint, is we friends, or is we ain't?"

I want to extend a special "thank you" to the Huntington City/Township Library, and the women that work so hard to make it an asset to the community. Their dedication in promoting local authors is an outstanding effort on their part. I will forever appreciate Deb, her support, and the author event she arranged on my behalf.

Edgil & Minnie "Griffith" Wicker with Clarence

Chapter I

The Wicker Family

AnnaBelle Wicker was born February 25, 1927 in Floyd County, Kentucky. She was the second child, and first daughter, of Edgil & Minnie "Griffith" Wicker. Shortly after her birth, came the Great Flood of 1927. This may have started her love of relocating. As you will find throughout this story, she loved the adventure of moving to new locations, and possessed the spirit to follow it through. I think it may have been heredity. Her father, my Grandpa, carried the gypsy spirit too, always a new dream, always a new endeavor.

Grandma and Grandpa would have fifteen children. Four of these children would not live past the age of three. They lost three daughters and one son. There was Margarette, who had polio, Lavinia, with double pneumonia, and Edgil Junior, he suffered with leukemia. The last little girl was stillborn, the cord wrapped around her tiny neck, she was the last baby Minnie would have. It's a great comfort to know they would all be waiting on Grandma and Grandpa to join them again later.

Mom spoke often of Margarette and Edgil Junior. These two had left the greatest impression on her young mind. Of course, being older, she took care of these children, so her memories were vivid. Margarette was probably around two when she passed away. It was determined at the time that she had polio; therefore she never learned to walk. Mom carried her everywhere. She said if you tried to hold her up to stand, she would scream in pain when there was any weight put upon her little legs. I have one picture of her sitting on a blanket outside; even in the photo you can see her suffering. She spoke of the Sunday morning she returned home from church with the other children to find the house full of people; even her Uncle Doctor was there. Edgil Jr. had taken a turn for the worse. She could still remember him standing in his crib screaming and

1

crying in pain as the blood vessels in his tiny body began to burst. This would be another memory that would never be forgotten, not by her, or her parents. Somehow, life continued after each loss.

The family's life in Kentucky was hectic, to say the least. Mom, and her older brother, Clarence, (nicknamed Bud), learned the meaning of hard work and discipline at a very early age. These two attributes would stay with them for life. This is not to say the other children didn't work, they did, but I know the responsibility that fell on the two oldest children.

The Wicker family was also full of love, fun, and adventure. They were all blessed with a sense of humor, it came directly from Grandpa. He used to tell Grandma they were raising a bunch of rodeo clowns. When I was a child, Grandma and Grandpa's house was my safe place, my favorite place, and the place I always wanted to be. I was lucky enough to be born to AnnaBelle, making it all possible for me.

But now, back to Mom. Her first crush was for one of the Mullins boys. Grandpa called him "warty ear"; he had famous nicknames for a lot of people over the years. Although this was an embarrassment for her, Mom said he did have warts on his ears. One thing that would not be tolerated was Mom having anything to do with a boy, so I guess the warts were the least of her worries.

AnnaBelle had a temper; it was well known to Bud (Clarence), and her younger brother, Ray. They both carried scars brought about by their sister. Bud carries his on his back, a victim of hot grease. Though his sister always regretted it, it didn't ease the pain at the time. She said it was just a reflex. She was about thirteen years old at the time, standing at the stove frying bacon for breakfast. They always had a big breakfast. Bud came into the kitchen from working in the fields, took off his shirt and washed up. He made the mistake of taking a piece of fried bacon that was cooling on a platter, when he turned to walk away she flipped a spoon of hot bacon grease on his back. Reflex? Sure, it was a reflex. It was the reflex of her "Wicker temper".

The "accident" that befell Ray came about when they were clearing a field of the rocks that could damage the plow blades. She said he just kept goofing off, teasing her, and generally being the nuisance he was well known to be. She finally snapped, he took off running to get away from her. She said that before she even had time to think, she threw a rock at him. For the one and only time in her life, the rock found its target, the back of his head. It seems he dropped like the rock that hit him. She thought she had killed him, so she ran up into the hills to hide, knowing her Daddy was going to kill her. They both lived. AnnaBelle tried to control her "reflexes", and the boy's tried to never turn their back on her.

Ray was the one child that would do anything on a dare, and almost anything without one. His uncles called him "Tut". The stories of his pranks followed him throughout his life. There was the time that his mother told him to go out and get that old hen off her nest. It seems she wouldn't quit sitting on her nest, not surprising, she was a "setting hen". But the eggs were to eat, not hatch. Ray not only got her off the nest, he poured gasoline on her, and set her on fire. She ran under the front porch of the house, flames and all, and came close to burning the place down. Through all the screaming and panic, they managed to get her from under the house, and put out the fire. It was a miracle, but the hen lived, never had another feather, but she lived. She also never sat on a nest again. So in his mind, Ray had done his job. In his mother's mind, he was lucky to be alive. His uncle once had a hunting dog that had a litter of pups. After they were weaned, he told Ray to get rid of them. I'm pretty sure he meant to find them a home. But Ray put them in a barrel, then rolled them down a hill. Unfortunately, the barrel hit a tree and killed all the puppies. This project didn't end well, for Ray or the puppies. But again, he felt he did as he was told. Try as he might, Edgil could never beat common sense into Ray. At least that's what he thought at the time. Ray would end up serving in the Air Force, owning his own business, and being a son that took care of his parents later in life. But he never lost that little boy charm, it carried him through life.

AnnaBelle loved school, something that was almost unheard of. She ended up missing a lot of days due to work at the house. She was a fast learner, and her lessons stayed with her, you would never have known her education was limited to the seventh grade.

She loved math, this would thankfully stay with her. She would need it for almost every venture she worked at in the future.

AnnaBelle was fourteen years old when they moved from Kentucky to Indiana in 1941. Her Grandfather Wicker had passed away that year. Before he died, he made his youngest son, Edgil, promise that he would take his growing family and move away from the hills of Kentucky. The coal mines were the only future left for his young grandsons, not much to look forward to. Mom used to speak of Hazzard, Kentucky, I guess we know why.

Even though the Wicker family had been fairly well off, and pillars in the community, Grandpa found himself in the mines. There seemed to be no other way to support his large family. He lost part of his second finger on his left hand in an accident at the coal mine, the dangers there were astronomical. He wanted something better for his sons.

Soon after the beginning of WW II the Kingsbury Munitions Plant was opened at LaPorte, Indiana. There, they produced shells, cartridges, and mortar rounds for the war. It was one of the largest munitions plants in the world. The place was huge, at one point they had 20,000 employees. This would be the new destination for the Wicker family. For AnnaBelle, this would be one of the best moves of her young life. Even though at the time, she didn't see the importance of leaving the hills of Kentucky behind. It was heartbreaking to leave the security of family and friends, only to move to what seemed like a flat, foreign land.

Before moving his family, Edgil made the first trip to Indiana by himself. He was determined to find work, and a place to bring his growing family. He ended staying with other family members who had already made the move. He found a job at Kingsbury. After three months of hard work and saving his money he was ready for his family to join him, he had rented a home for them not far from LaPorte, at Medaryville, Indiana..

The trip north to Indiana proved to be quite a chore. AnnaBelle and Bud helped their Mother with the burden of packing, and running after their six little siblings. When they left Kentucky, they drove straight through to LaPorte. It was early 1942, still winter, and very cold. AnnaBelle was lucky enough to sit in the front cab of the truck with her Mother and help with the baby. The other seven children were in the back of the canvas covered truck. They had lined the walls of the vehicle with the mattresses, more for warmth than comfort. The trip was uneventful but for one little error on the part of Ray, not a shock to anyone who knew him. They had what was called a "slop jar" in the back of the truck for the kids to "relieve themselves". At one point, the odor was becoming unbearable. Ray decided to empty it, opening the canvas flap on the back of the truck and dumping out the contents. Unfortunately, they were coming around the circle in downtown Indianapolis at the time. The only thing that saved them was that they were still in the darkness of early morning, no one else was out and about. The first arrivals that day were in for a rude awakening, really rude.

They finally arrived in Medaryville, no worse for wear. They settled in their new home, a nice house with a park across the street for the kids to play. Life was much better for them all. Bud joined the Navy when he was seventeen in the early months of 1942. AnnaBelle started working at the Kingsbury plant, along with her father, shortly after her brother went to war. Her age didn't seem to matter, they needed workers. She wore the white coveralls like everyone else, and worked long, hard hours. The pay was good, and the family always needed the extra money.

Shortly before Bud joined the Navy, he decided he would teach AnnaBelle how to drive the family car. He took her down the road, away from the house. She drove a short distance, and didn't do too badly, it was going well. He told her to drive back to the house and they would show their father that she could handle the car. As she turned slowly into the driveway about six of her young siblings jumped on the car. They were on the hood, the running boards, hanging on the doors, they seemed to be everywhere. For some unknown reason, AnnaBelle panicked, her foot pressed down hard on the gas, instead of the brake. The car accelerated, hit the house, and children flew in every direction. I guess they showed their Dad, unfortunately, it wasn't what he wanted to see. On the up side, not one of the "little fools" was seriously hurt. On the down side, AnnaBelle's confidence took a beating, she swore she would never drive again.

AnnaBelle was raised in a good, clean home. Her mother taught her the importance of cleanliness, and the ability to cook for a large family. Minnie and Edgil both worked very hard to support and care for their large family. I think they were wonderful. They would end up raising eleven children. In order of birth they were: Clarence, AnnaBelle, Raymond, Martha, Donald, James, Linda, Annis Lee, Harold, Douglas, and Janet.

I know in my heart that the Grandpa I knew and loved was not the father the older children knew and loved. I've been told he was a strict disciplinarian, not afraid to use his belt when he felt it was necessary. He never once raised his voice or his hand to me. Now, Grandma on the other hand, could wield a wicked switch. One she would make you pick yourself from the various bushes in the yard. God forbid you bring back something that wasn't big enough to really sting. The one thing you didn't want was Grandma picking the switch. As I look back, how she kept her sanity with all of us is beyond me. As a child and teenager, I never realized the extra burden of work my sister and I added to Grandma's life, I only knew I wanted to be with them. I will forever be grateful for the generosity and love of my Grandparents.

Grandpa was a story teller (he should have been the writer). When I was little, I hung on his every word. That never really changed, the stories did, but not the hanging on. I must have been around four years old, and staying with my Grandparents in Lowell, when he told me the story about the old lady in Kentucky that was missing one of her thumbs. We were raised during the era of the "outhouse". I hated that strange little building, and would put off going there as long as possible. It was not only scary, but in the spring and summer, it housed spiders, wasps, and God knows what else. To add to my fear, Grandpa told me that when I went #2, I had to be sure and not get any poop on me when I wiped myself. He said there was no way to get it off your hands, no amount of soap would clean it. (I know it's gross, but please bear with me. There is just no other way to effectively say it.) Anyway, he said there was this old lady that got some on her thumb, and they had to cut it off. Then he held up the stump of his middle finger on his left hand. (The one he actually lost in the coal mines.) He explained to me in detail how that finger was sacrificed because he failed to take the time to wipe properly. I was terrified. I wouldn't go until my eyes were crossing and I couldn't walk upright. It was bad, really bad. But worse than bad was that he never told me any different. No, it's not good English, but it works for me.

The best part of that story was something I found out years later, on one of my visits to Florida. My Uncle Jim relayed this to me about ten years ago when Mom and I went to his house for supper at St. Pete. He said that one thing he remembered about my stepdad, Stovall, was that he constantly "bitched" about the amount of toilet paper that we used. He couldn't understand how two little girls could go through so many rolls in one week. That brought about the first time I told anyone, including Mom, about the #2, the old lady, her lost thumb, Grandpa's partly missing digit, and the story he told me. They laughed for hours that night, reliving Grandpa's stories. Mom did say that would explain my stomach problems, and the reason for the weekly castor oil. God, I hated that stuff. She would wait until I was in the bathtub, trapped, with no way to escape. Here she came with that ugly bottle and the nasty tasting stuff it held, I had to take it.

One of Grandpa's cutest quotes was about a street in Wayland, Kentucky. It was named Push & Plum Street. If you pushed your head out the window, you were plum out of town. And the story about the family at dinner with the last pork chop. He said there were fourteen children in the family, they were all seated at the dinner table. There was only one pork chop left on the platter. Just as the old man reached for it, the lights went out. When they came back on, he had fourteen forks stuck in his hand. Come on, that's funny stuff.

Life at Grandma and Grandpa's house was nothing short of wonderful for me, it held everything I could have wanted. There was always love, my favorite aunts and uncles, good food, a warm bed, and the security of knowing they would always be there.

AnnaBelle 1934

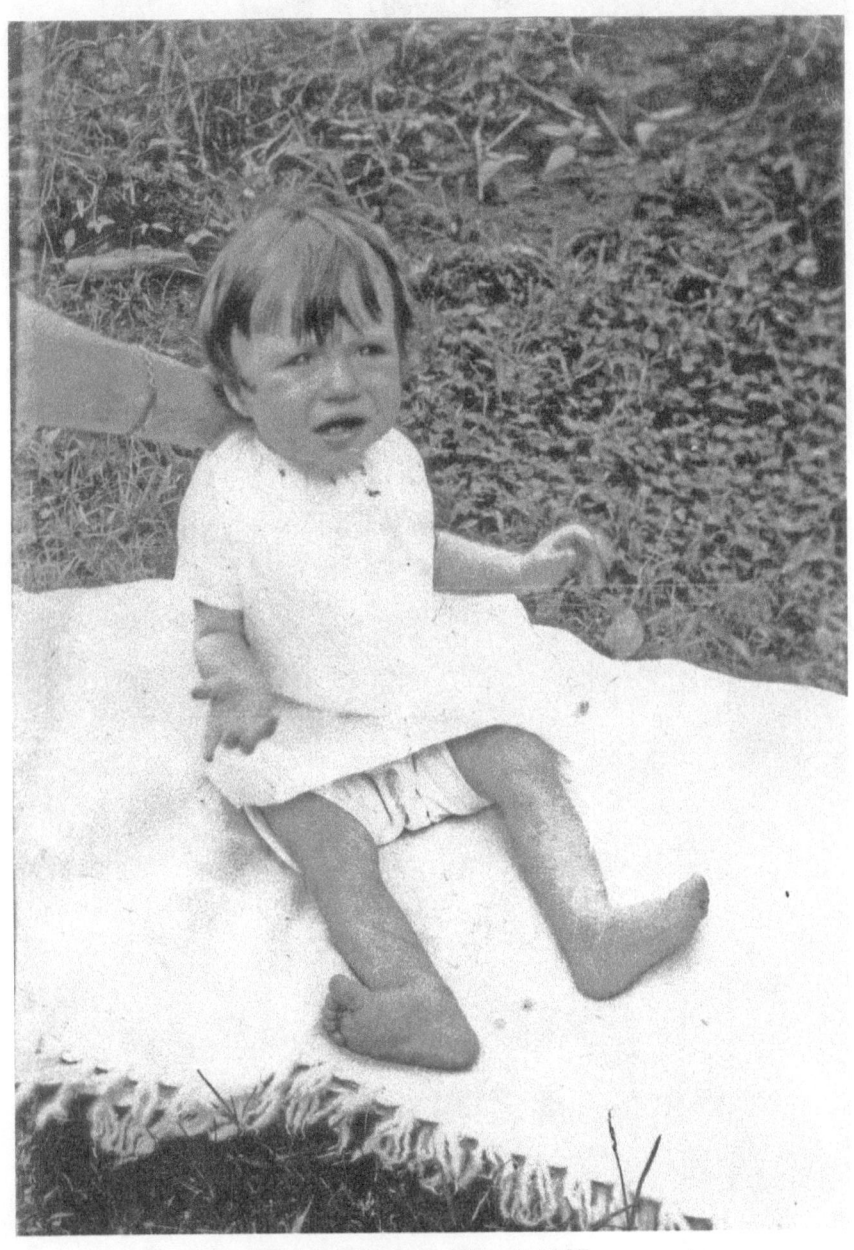

Margarette (Circa) 1937

1941
Top: Minnie and Millie (Davis) Wicker , (Edgil's Mother)
Center: AnnaBelle and Clarence holding Annis Lee,
Bottom: Don and Ray

The Brothers & Sisters   Early 1980's
From Left:
Ray, AnnaBelle, Jim, Linda, Harold, Janet, Bud, Annis Lee,
Doug,
Martha, and Don

Edgil and Minnie   1965

Chapter II

From Wicker To Bollan

AnnaBelle met Don Bollan in 1945. At least she would know him as Don. This was not his real name, but later she would learn why he felt the need to use an alias, and that his given name was David Otto. It wouldn't be in time to save their marriage, it would, however, be part of the reason it ended. She was working at the restaurant that my grandparents leased and operated at the time. She was always an excellent cook, and obviously a good waitress. He was a truck driver, stopped at the restaurant often, and fell in love with Mom. I'm not sure how my grandparents felt about the blossoming romance. He was nine years her junior, had been married, with three children, and was now divorced. The divorced part turned out to be a lie, the marriage and three children part, very true. But, she was eighteen, and he was quite the talker.

Everyone liked Don, he played the guitar, he sang, he liked to party at times, and he was full of charisma. Being tall and good looking didn't hurt either. He was well over six feet tall, she was five foot, and they both had blue eyes. AnnaBelle was beautiful in her own right. She had inherited her smile and black curly hair from her father and the Wicker family.

AnnaBelle and Don were married in June, 1945. Thus began the marriage that would produce two daughters, four years of conflict, and the power of love tested to the end. They had a stormy relationship, but not until the deceit and lies emerged did it truly fall apart.

When they were first married they lived with AnnaBelle's parents for a while. Almost the entire family (In-laws and outlaws.) lived with Edgil and Minnie at one time or another. Mom told me her and Dad were asked to leave because of something Dad had done. I do know what it was now, and so does the person that helped to cause it, but I know Mom wouldn't want me to say.

What I will say, is this much, I am not as forgiving as Mom was. I may never forgive her for hurting the one person that loved them all so much. It wouldn't be the last time this same person brought great pain to AnnaBelle.

Nothing in this world meant as much to AnnaBelle as her parents did at that time. Probably, not even her husband. She was pregnant with her first child, and their first grandchild, the timing could not have been worse. Nothing that is, except the thought of her parents not wanting to see, or speak to her.

She and Don lived in his car until he could afford a small apartment. It was winter, a very cold one at that. They finally moved into a tiny little place, it was upstairs. She was blessed to have a caring landlady that lived downstairs.

AnnaBelle gave birth to her first daughter on March 6, 1946, her husband named the baby Katheryn Ann. They called her Kathy. What should have been the most beautiful day of her young life was marred by the absence of her parents. It affected both her and her baby.

Once she arrived home with her new baby, reality set in quickly. Kathy cried constantly. AnnaBelle feared she had somehow marked the baby with her own tears over the absence of her parents. She walked the floor with this crying child, who never slept more than a couple of short hours at a time. Finally, her sweet landlady came to her rescue. She heard the pacing and came upstairs to help. She would rock the baby into silence so that her mother could sleep for a while. It was exhausting.

When Kathy was about three months old AnnaBelle's parents finally gave in and came to see their daughter and first grandchild. (A child that was still crying.) The grandfather knew at once what was wrong, the baby was starving. He went to the store, bought bottles, milk, and dark Karo syrup. He returned, fixed a bottle, fed the baby, and laid her down. To everyone's surprise, the child slept sound for over eight hours. Her father had been right, AnnaBelle's milk wasn't good for her baby, the baby was hungry, and a little skinny. It seems unlikely this could happen after tending to all those siblings she had, but her mother had never faced this problem.

Life moved forward, at least she had her parents back. Don was still driving a truck, and on the road a lot, but things were better. AnnaBelle found herself pregnant again when Kathy was four months old. Even though she wanted a large family like her parents, this wasn't the best timing in the world. Her first labor and delivery were very hard on her, taking over twenty four hours. The nurses ending up giving her castor oil and having her husband try to walk her up and down the aisle. The first birth is hard enough on any woman, let alone one with such a small frame.

Before her second baby was due to be born, AnnaBelle's older brother, Bud, was discharged from the Navy. The war was over; it was time for everyone to move on with their lives. She would need help with Kathy when she went to the hospital to have the new baby, at that time women spent two weeks in the hospital after giving birth. Don decided to make the trip to Missouri and bring his youngest sister, Darlene, to Indiana to stay with them for a while, she could care for Katheryn while AnnaBelle was absent. Bud decided to go along for the ride. This would end up being a life changing trip for him and Darlene both. They fell in love and were married four months later.

AnnaBelle gave birth to her second daughter on April 14, 1947, her husband named this child Carolyn Sue. This delivery was so much easier than the first, surprisingly, they usually are. This baby thrived, turning into a happy, healthy, chubby, little child. She was so unlike her sister. AnnaBelle and her two daughters would share a bond in life known only by a few. Circumstances would lead them in many directions, to many places, and with many people. AnnaBelle would never have the large family she wanted, but in the end, she would have the two daughters she needed.

By the year 1949 AnnaBelle and Don had leased a restaurant on Highway 41, about two miles outside of Lowell, Indiana. They appropriately named it "AnnaBelle's". Since Don was still driving a semi, the business was left to his wife. This was fine with her; she loved a challenge, and the hard work that went along with it. Being slightly ambitious helped with the work load too, she was determined to succeed, and have the things in life that she had always dreamed of. She never had more than two employees. Family also helped with the business. Bud and Darlene spent many weekends working and helping out. During the week they were both working at the Kingsbury Munitions Plant. Bud had been called back by the military after the end of the war. He worked in the testing and development of weapons. But on the weekends, they both loved being a part of the hustle and bustle at AnnaBelle's, it was a busy place.

There were living quarters in the back of the building, a nice two bedroom apartment. It was just the right size for the small family. This gave her the freedom to start her days very early in the morning. She was able to take care of the restaurant with the peace of mind that came with knowing her daughters were only a few steps away at any given moment.

Bud and Darlene spent most of their free time with Don and AnnaBelle. Both sets of brothers and sisters were very close. The four of them would go out every Saturday night. Everything went well until Don had a few too many drinks, then all he wanted to do was fight. Because he drank a lot, this happened almost every time they went out, well, actually every Saturday night. He was a pretty good fighter, but some nights he was too drunk to carry it off. Then, of course, Bud thought he could help, so they both ended up fighting half the bar. There were always the usual wounds, cuts, blood, and bruises. However, there was one night when one man's wife put a beer bottle in her purse, swung it at Don's head, connected, knocking him out cold. Of course there was screaming and panic, the girls thought he was dead. He lived, but with a major headache. However, it wasn't bad enough to stop him from returning the following weekend.

AnnaBelle began her day at 2 A.M. with the preparation of her famous cinnamon rolls and other desserts. Her clientele consisted of people from all walks of life. Families, businessmen, travelers, and the truck drivers that loved the home cooking she served. The drivers would end up being her allies in the war against her husband's infidelity, the infidelity she never suspected.

The truck drivers that frequented the restaurant had a fondness for AnnaBelle. They liked Don too, everyone did. They knew how hard she worked, and they also knew that Don was fooling around in more than one place. The men talked it over and decided they had to tell her what her husband was doing behind her back. They were men, but even they had become tired of him not appreciating what he had at home.

When they first confronted her about his wanderings, she wouldn't even hear of it, calling them liars and becoming very angry with them. They let it go, they knew they had planted the seeds of doubt in her mind. Sadly, it was true, they had. She had always trusted him completely, it never occurred to her that he would be unfaithful.

Not long after their first attempt, two of the drivers came in one evening and decided to approach her once more with the facts about her husband. They begged her to go with them, and they would prove it to her. Although it was the last thing she wanted to do, she got in the truck and went. A few miles down the road at a motel, sat his truck. She went in, found him with not one, but two, women. A mother and her daughter, no less. They owned the motel. The shock, the hurt, the disbelief, all of it was more than she thought she could bear, but, bear it she did. Don must have thought his wife would never catch him. He knew she trusted him, he also knew she could not drive and follow him. She had never learned to drive. This would be her biggest regret in life, never knowing the freedom to come and go on her own. She had to depend on others.

The first thing she did was take her two and three year old daughters, and move in with her parents. They lived a couple of miles from the restaurant, she had decided she could commute. This didn't set well with her husband, his way with words wasn't helping him this time. He loved her more than anything in the world, he was getting angry because she wouldn't listen to reason. One night he not only bought a bottle and got drunk, he decided to go bring her home at gunpoint. When he arrived at the house and she refused to go with him, his anger increased. Finally, Edgil had no choice, he ordered him off the property. He got as far as his car when his anger turned to rage, Don began firing shots at the house, breaking windows and putting holes in the walls. As everyone lay on the floor in the dark, to avoid getting hit by a stray bullet, somehow Edgil found the phone and managed to call the police. Luckily, there were no physical injuries. I'm sure it left some mental trauma, but nothing permanent.

Not long after the shooting incident, he somehow talked AnnaBelle into going back home with him to the restaurant. I'm sure her biggest concern was for the business she had worked so hard to build. Things would never be the same between the two of them, so eventually their relationship was doomed to failure. She could never find it in her heart to trust him again. But then, who could?

David Otto Bollan   1938

Otto & AnnaBelle   1947

Bud & Darlene   1947

From Left:
Darlene "Bollan" Wicker, Lillie "Bollan" Little,
AnnaBelle "Wicker" Bollan 1950

David Otto Bollan (With his Hudson)   1950

AnnaBelle's Restaurant   1950
(With her business card.)

Carolyn, Daddy, and Kathy   1950
(In back of AnnaBelle's.)

Carolyn and Kathy   1949

Kathy and Carolyn   1950
(AnnaBelle's Banana Curls Girls)

Chapter III

THE BATTLE BEGINS.....THE DREAMS SOON

END

Don introduced AnnaBelle to his first wife Willodean, and the three children, about three years into their marriage. It would be the infamous trip to Missouri that would bring them all together. Why she agreed to this trip was something that she, herself, failed to realize. It was not in her nature to just go along with things. It was shortly after she learned about his cheating, so perhaps she didn't have the will to fight it. At any rate, for some unknown reason, Don felt the need to take all of them, in his big Hudson, on a trip home.

The three grownups were in the front seat, with AnnaBelle in the middle. The five children lined up across the backseat in order of their ages, the eldest on one side, and the youngest on the other. Don, Ted, Janelle, Katheryn, and Carolyn. Here was another Don Bollan, perhaps AnnaBelle thought he was a junior. He wasn't, but I'm sure that's what she told herself.

The trip was a nightmare for her, as each trip to Missouri ended up being. Don chose to go in town to the bar every night they were there. AnnaBelle stayed at the house, tending to her daughters. But worse than him being gone was her being left with the "mother-in-law," Effie. She didn't like AnnaBelle, and in no way did she try to hide it.

Alma Effie Thomas was born February 21, 1891 in Ozark County, Missouri. She would marry William Henry Bollan in 1907 or 1908, William was born March 3, 1886 in Letcher, Kentucky. They would have ten children together, Fred, Freelove, Mary, Leneve, David Otto, Lillie, Everett, Bonnie, Darlene, and Billie. They would lose Mary at the age of nine due to an accident. It was a terrible situation at the time, Effie never recovered from the grief of her loss. Mary had fell and hit her head, back then, there wasn't medical help readily available. The wound healed in the beginning, at least on the outside. Later, the hole began to fester and infection set in. it wasn't long until Mary passed away. Effie kept her daughter's hair in a long braid, and when Mary died, Effie cut the braid off and kept it. Even after sixteen years, Darlene can remember seeing her mother cry for hours while holding the braid. This grieving went on for years, until the braid disappeared. It was thought Effie's husband, William, finally either destroyed the braid, or put it away someplace where his wife couldn't find it. The entire family wanted this bizarre behavior to stop, and stop it finally did. Mary's braid was never found again. To this day no one really knows what happened to it.

It has been difficult tracing the family roots for William Henry Bollan, due to the fact that he was born out of wedlock. His mother, Mary, moved to Missouri when he was very young. She had yet another child out-of-wedlock, a daughter, before she would marry. It is believed William was given his mother's maiden name because his father was already married to another woman at the time of his birth. In the 1800's this had to be a stigma that was difficult to live with, it may have been the reason she took her young son and left the state. This story will be fascinating when all the facts can be uncovered. There are roots for the Bollan name in Scotland, England, and Ireland, including several with the same name, William Henry Bollan. It will be interesting to see where this leads.

David Otto Bollan was born April 15, 1918, in Ozark, Missouri. He was the fifth child and second son of Effie and William, he would be known as Otto. He left home at the age of fourteen due the treatment he received from his mother. He soon returned and stayed until the age of seventeen. At this time Otto joined the Civilian Conservation Corp (CCC), the year was 1935. This program was enacted on March 21, 1933, it was the first recovery and relief bill submitted to Congress by President Franklin D. Roosevelt after the Great Depression.

The CCC was set up for young men ages 17 to 25. They were paid $30.00 per month. Of this, they were required to send $25.00 home to their family. Food and lodging were furnished, along with medical care. The program ended in 1942, due to W.W. II. The program, and the men involved, helped to make our national parks what they are today. Otto worked on various projects in Missouri. These included Bennett Springs, and the Bagnel Dam. After leaving the CCC program, he worked cutting and hauling cedar logs to Indiana. Here, he met Willodean, through her brother, and ended up staying. (Well, for a while.) Back to the story at hand.

As stated earlier, Effie never liked AnnaBelle, probably because she was so fond of Willodean. She had to blame someone for her son's behavior, so it fell on the second wife. She, herself should have carried some of the blame, because of the way she treated her children. She deeply loved her family, but she could be a very cold woman at times. This may have accounted for the bad behavior that would eventually surface in her son. In later years she would defend this son with a vengeance. Perhaps she realized how her actions may have helped lead to his downfall.

And now, back to the trip. It's still a mystery as to why no one slipped up that weekend. No one mentioned Don's name wasn't Don, and, he had never divorced Willodean. But the worst deceit ended up being that everyone knew his secret, except AnnaBelle. In the end, they weren't really doing him a favor. There's that tangled web thing he was weaving, weaving, weaving, but eventually that began to fall apart.

It wasn't long after this trip, that AnnaBelle and Don closed the restaurant at Lowell and opened one at Remington, Indiana. It was located on Highway 24, south of their first location. This would be their last home together. The relationship never recovered after she found him at the motel that night. It never would. His drinking also became a serious issue.

Don took his two small daughters almost everywhere he went, except when he was working on the road. Then the day came that Katheryn pulled the bottle of whiskey from under the seat, in front of her mother. AnnaBelle had warned him to never drink with the girls in the car, so, that was the end of their rides with Daddy. She had been with him in the car when he was drunk, he had come close to killing them all more than once. There were times when he was drinking that he would sit Kathy on his lap and let her steer the car, she was no more than four years old. There was no power steering back then, and that Hudson was like driving a tank. The more AnnaBelle screamed at him, the faster he would go. Even though he was an excellent driver when he was sober, she couldn't risk the lives of her daughters. He could no longer be trusted.

She never had the joy or hope at this restaurant that she thrived on at "AnnaBelle's". Don had not only broken her heart, he had broken her spirit. She knew they would never have the things in life she had planned and worked so hard for. His drinking had started to control him, he was no longer controlling the bottle, or anything else in his life. It wasn't long before fate stepped in. I truly believe there is a point at which God will step into the situation and say.....enough.

Don's downfall came on a night like any other, he came back to the restaurant drinking. He was already drunk. They had an altercation, he took all the money, and left. AnnaBelle closed the restaurant that evening because she had no cash on hand to run with. Little did she know this would be her last and final closing. Furthermore, she had no idea that her life was going to take the first turn down a very twisted road.

As Don left Remington, driving east, the police started what would be the chase of a lifetime, at least for them. His driving was erratic, it was obvious he was drinking. They couldn't overcome the speed of the Hudson, evidently Don knew they never would, he made no attempt to slow down. The police never gave up the pursuit, they chased him for almost fifty miles. Through the towns of Monticello, Logansport, and Peru, never leaving Highway 24. Don was a truck driver, he knew the road like the back of his hand, and this was his advantage. Luckily, it was late at night, and traffic was light, it was a miracle no one was killed.

Finally, in desperation, his pursuers radioed ahead to the state police. They in turn had the foresight to set up a roadblock at

Wabash. This was how they stopped him, this is how life as he had known it, would end.

In the meantime, AnnaBelle, oblivious to all of it, had made her own decision that night. She took her two small daughters to the neighbor's house to spend the night. She returned to the restaurant, took a butcher knife from the kitchen, and went upstairs to bed, where she would wait for her husbands return. Her mind was set, one of them would be dead by morning. When he returned, she was prepared to put an end to the hurt and deceit of the last five years. It would have been like David and Goliath, he was 6'3", she at 5'. She was going to see how mighty the sword would be. How far can one human be pushed before the inevitable happens, they start to push back? AnnaBelle was finding out.

Even though Don was probably headed to Wabash anyway that night, he wouldn't go farther that the city limits before he and his Hudson were pulled over. Wabash was the home of his first wife, Willodean, and their three children. I'm sure he had been there many times over the years without AnnaBelle's knowledge. Sadly, this was the one time she wouldn't have cared anyway. Unbelievably, she had fallen asleep during the night, with the knife at her side.

AnnaBelle was awakened by the ringing of the phone at daylight the next morning. Half asleep she jumped up, and ran down the steps to answer it. When she heard the Wabash police department on the other end of the line, she was instantly alert. They told her they had her husband in custody, and asked if she wanted to post bail for him. She politely told them to keep him, and hung up. Could he have been crazy enough to think for one minute that she would come to his rescue and bail him out? With what? In the end, it didn't matter, she was done with him, and done with his lies.

After Don was arrested, they found he had an outstanding warrant for back child support. Then things began to unravel for him. It finally came to light that he was still married to Willodean. AnnaBelle would soon learn that she was never legally married. Within a matter of day's she would also learn his name wasn't

Don, it was David Otto Bollan, and his family called him Otto. There was only one Don Bollan, and that was his oldest son. It seems he had started using his son's name when he married her, just to avoid detection.

While her husband sat in jail facing various charges, AnnaBelle had her own battles to fight. Otto had left her with a lease she couldn't fulfill, a mountain of debt, no money, and two little girls. There was also the broken heart, beaten spirit, and the lost dreams. She had no choice in her destination; she would have to go home to her parents.

It took a while, but finally AnnaBelle had all her belongings packed. She and her daughters were waiting for her Daddy, Edgil, to pick them up and take them home with him. Before he arrived, her landlord pulled into the parking lot. He informed her that Otto currently owed him four hundred dollars and he wasn't letting her take her furniture until he was repaid. He knew the circumstances, he knew she had no money, but he also knew she had very nice furnishings. She was crying when Edgil arrived with the truck. He wasn't happy about his son-in-law anyway; this man picked the wrong day to mess with the Wicker family. It never came to blows, but they left with the furniture. Her Dad was right, AnnaBelle didn't borrow the money, and she wasn't paying it back. The guy could try to intimidate someone else's daughter.

She settled in at her parent's home with "the girls", they would always be "the girls". She had fought very hard to have a solid, independent future, but without the help and support of her husband, she watched those dreams go up in smoke. As much as she loved her family, this wasn't where she wanted to be. They already carried a huge responsibility with eight children still at home, now there were a total of thirteen people to be cared for. She was determined to try and get her life straightened out.

There were legal battles to be fought; AnnaBelle had to hire a lawyer. Because she was never legally married to Otto, the marriage was annulled. How can they just annul five years of your life? For the five years she thought they were legally man and wife, it turned out they were actually in a common law marriage. What would be known as "living together" in today's world. The worst part of the battle was yet to be fought. In the eyes of the law, her two daughters were illegitimate. She really began to hate Otto for what he had left her with. There was a court hearing; the judge ruled in her favor, the girls would legally carry the Bollan name.

I have to interject some facts here, just to clarify the story. I recently made the drive to Wabash and went to the court house. In the records department of the circuit court they had the transcripts for the various charges and eventual trial of David Otto Bollan. Everything had been transferred to microfilm. I had them make copies of the films and left with them. I wanted to read through the contents at home, where I could be comfortable. In hind site, I wish I had done this before I wrote the first book; it represented a different aspect of the man that was my father.

According to the paperwork, Willodean had filed charges against Dad three times in the years from 1939 to 1945 for neglect to support his wife and children. In 1939 there was only one child, Don. In 1943 there were two children, Don and Ted. The final charges were in April of 1945. By this time there were three minor children, Don, Ted, and Janelle. It seems evident that he was absent from the marriage for the most part, going home long enough to have another child. I can't say that I understand her reasoning, but I can say that I wasn't the one in love with him.

The actual trial took place in 1952. He had served time at the jail for the charges of driving under the influence. The charges facing him at the trial were strictly "failure to pay support". It was during the question and answer period that it came to light that he had filed for divorce against Willodean in 1945. She cross filed and he agreed to let her go through with the finalization. He paid her attorney fees and left Wabash, thinking he was free to marry AnnaBelle. He didn't know Willodean had dropped the divorce after he left. To my utter surprise, I found he was telling the truth, he believed he was free to re-marry. Which he did, he married AnnaBelle the following June. I always believed he was sent to prison for bigamy, he was not. According to the paperwork,

Willodean told the court that Otto didn't know she had dropped the divorce proceeding's.

As the trial ended, the court found him guilty of non support for his minor children. They showed him no mercy, because the charges had been on-going for so long. He was sentenced to no less than one year, and no more than seven years at the Indiana State Prison. In the end, he served the minimum of one year.

Indiana State Prison is located in Michigan City, Indiana. As I have said, when he was sober you couldn't ask for a better person, and sober he was for that entire year. Having no access to alcohol made him the model prisoner. Since he was athletic, he became the pitcher for the baseball team. Bud and Darlene would go watch the games on the week-ends when they could. They observed from outside the tall chain link fence, but still had a good view. He would be allowed to come to the fence to talk to them for a few minutes after the game. The only thing he ever asked them for was coffee. He told them where they could leave it outside the fence. He didn't really want the coffee, but he could trade it for cigarettes. So each time they went, they would take him a pound of coffee.

I remember being at the prison, but only once, Kathy and I must have went with Uncle Bud and Aunt Darlene, I know for sure it couldn't have been any one else. He was out in the yard, but behind a fence, I can remember how happy he was to see us. I know Mom gave them the needed permission, it had to be shortly before she married Stovall. He would not have allowed us any contact with the man we called Daddy.

Shortly after the conviction of her son, AnnaBelle's ex mother-in-law, Effie, came to Indiana with an attitude and a mission. She went to the Wicker house with every intention of taking her two little granddaughters away from their mother, and back to Missouri with her. Her hatred for AnnaBelle, and her anger about her son be imprisoned, drove her like a mad person. She was blind to the fact that Otto had left five children and two women with no visible means of support, and their lives in shambles.

When Effie, her husband, William, and their youngest son, Billy arrived at the Wicker home, they were not really prepared *for Edgil. He may have seemed like a mild, quiet man to them, but this was not the man they faced that day. One thing he would not tolerate was someone hurting one of his children, and now he would fight for his two granddaughters as well. Effie was screaming and accusing, she said AnnaBelle wasn't fit to raise the girls. This was the final straw for Edgil, he ordered them off his property before he had to resort to "beating the shit out of them". He told Effie she had better go back to Missouri and stay there.*

What made this whole situation so ironic was the fact that Effie had accused AnnaBelle of messing around on her son, and that the youngest girl, Carolyn, did not belong to Otto. Katheryn could not be denied, she looked like her father, there could be no doubt, this child was a Bollan. Carolyn, on the other hand favored her mother and the Wickers. After accusing AnnaBelle of this for years, now she wanted her granddaughters.

It was shortly after this incident that AnnaBelle went to pieces, had a breakdown, and was sent away to "rest" for a few weeks. She was sent to a facility in northern Indiana at Westville. Her daughters would remain with their grandparents until she could once again care for them. The doctors and staff at Westville were supportive and kind. Her recovery was quick, she was still a strong willed person. Finally, she felt well enough to return to her parents, daughters, and the new life she was facing.

Chapter IV

ONE BATTLE ENDS..... THEN STOVALL BEGINS

AnnaBelle started working at one of the restaurants at Lowell. There was a truck driver that started coming in regularly, his name was Jim Stovall. She had known him before, when she had AnnaBelle's Restaurant outside Lowell on Highway 41. Of course he was nice, of course he was charming, and of course, he had hated Otto Bollan. One is forced to think that this man knew when to make his move, as it turned out, he had wanted her for years.

No one really knows for sure what drove her into his arms, could it have been love? Or did he offer all the things that she so desperately needed. A home, security, and place for her and her two girls to live. This would take some of the burden off of her parents. For whatever reason, she took the girls and moved to Lafayette, Indiana with Jim. He rented a small apartment for them to live in, and worked to support her and her daughters.

For the first time in her life, AnnaBelle had the security of her own home, without the worry of money. She continued to suffer with bouts of sever depression. At these times Katheryn and Carolyn would return to Grandma and Grandpas to "visit". This was fine with the girls. From a very early age, this was where they always felt safe and at home. That would never change.

By the time the girls started school, AnnaBelle and Jim were formally married. They had re-located back to Lowell. He found his new wife never liked being too far from her family. He was from Boswell, Indiana, his parents lived there, with the rest of their children in close proximity. This time AnnaBelle's in-laws liked her, and loved the girls. Actually, one night Jim's dad tried to like her a little too much, always a battle to be fought. She said later that the "crazy" old man came right to the bed she and Jim were sleeping in and started groping her. He only tried it once, didn't succeed, so he let it go. In the end, she would find the apple didn't fall far from the tree in that family.

Life continued in a fairly routine manner for a couple of years. There were things about her husband she began to notice that didn't seem quite normal, but she brushed it aside. He loved her, and seemed to love her daughters very much, everyone seemed to be so impressed with this, the perfect little family.

When they were first married he always managed to be in the room after the girls had their baths. They would run to their mom, she had their clothes, and would help them dress. The only one comfortable with this practice was Jim. Neither of the girls wanted to be in front of this man without clothes on. He was always there, they never seemed to be able to have a private moment with their mom. AnnaBelle soon sensed there was a problem, and the practice stopped. She would come to the bathroom to help them dress.

He had the girls start washing dishes and cleaning before they could reach the sink, they would stand on a stool. This was common, most kids did in the 1950's. One girl washed the dishes, the other dried, they alternated every other week. This was a good routine, there was never an argument over who did what. When they finished the dishes, one would sweep the floor, the other took out the trash. He always told them that if he found food or anything on the dishes or silverware, he would take everything out of the cabinets and make them wash and dry it all. Pots, pans, dishes, silverware, and baking pans, when he said everything, he meant it. It was a lesson well taught, it only took once for them to learn it. It seemed a little harsh for six and seven year olds, but it worked. Their mother didn't like it, but she didn't argue about it. Needless to say, the dishes were always clean.

In 1954 the family moved to Valparaiso. AnnaBelle loved it here. This is where she lived with Otto when they were first married, this is where her children were born. It was a great little town, there was always something to do, the people were friendly and nice. They would move three times in the three years they remained in Valpo, but the girls never had to change schools. Did I say, AnnaBelle and her restless spirit loved new places? Since they had married, five years earlier, she and Jim had lived in four different towns. This would be the longest period the girls would ever attend one school, three years in a row was the record.

The day came when Otto was released from prison. He was devastated to find AnnaBelle had remarried, and who it was that she married. It seems he hated Jim Stovall as much as Jim hated him. He had written so many letters begging AnnaBelle to wait for him, professing his love for her and their daughters. Of this, there was never any doubt, her doubt lay with the fact he had lied to her, and betrayed her. She could never get past the hurt, even though he continued to swear that he thought he was divorced. AnnaBelle did the worst possible thing she could to Otto, she took away his right to see his two small daughters. She couldn't trust him with his drinking, and she wasn't putting the girls through anything else. Even though he wasn't allowed to talk to his daughters, he did park his car on a side street so he could watch them walk to school in the mornings. The girls noticed the car, and the man watching them, but it never crossed their young minds to question who it could be, or what he might be looking for. They would find out years later this man was their father.

David Otto Bollan was killed in a car accident at 4:15 PM on Saturday, May 26, 1956. He was 38 years old. According to the newspaper, three people were killed instantly when their car was struck by a speeding New York Central passenger train. In the car with Otto were, Mrs. Ruth Brown, 22, and her infant daughter Kathryn, 6 months old. The accident happened at the Babcock Road crossing at Chesterton, Indiana. The crossing was unguarded by gates or signals and stands on a rise of ground, making it hard to see oncoming trains until one is "on top" of the crossing. Mrs. Brown was separated from her husband. It was believed Mr. Bollan was taking her to work. After the accident, the fireman on the train told a Mr. Elmer Johnson that Mrs. Brown seemed to see the train before Bollan. The last glimpse of the cars occupants showed Mrs. Brown frantically clutching her baby to her chest.

It was at this point in the story that my memories began to blend with Mom's. I was nine years old when Dad was killed.

The day Mom received the phone call is a day that is etched in my memory. We were living at 501 Freeman Street in Valparaiso, we were living in the downstairs apartment. It was located across the street from the oldest area of the Valparaiso University Campus. Even in the 1950's the buildings there were old, but majestically beautiful. I loved riding my bicycle around the area.

It was Monday, May 28ᵗʰ around 5 PM when Mom received the phone call about Dad's death. Kathy and I were sitting on the floor watching the Mickey Mouse Club show, Mom was ironing clothes. When she hung up the phone, she collapsed in tears against the wall. She sobbed and cried for what seemed like an eternity, at least to the two of us. We went to her, but didn't know what to do, or why we should do it. When she finally composed herself, she told us our Dad had been killed in an accident. Silently, all three of us knew it was a blessing that Jim Stovall wasn't home to see the display of emotion.

Once again, Mom found herself face to face with a very hurt and angry Effie Bollan. Kathy and I had not seen our Grandma and Grandpa Bollan for years. Luckily, we were both at school the day they came to see Mom. That would not have been a good memory for either of us to have. They had once again made the trip from Missouri to Indiana, this time to claim the body of their son, he would be buried in Missouri. She came knocking on the apartment door one afternoon, demanding Mom turn Kathy and I over to her. Of course that wasn't going to happen, so then the screaming and accusing started anew. And yet again, she left in a rage, leaving a distraught and crying AnnaBelle standing in the doorway. Grandpa Bollan returned alone the next morning to apologize to Mom for what his wife had said and done. Mom said he was one of the kindest people she had ever met. Opposites do attract.

Mom didn't hear anymore from Grandma Bollan until there was a hearing set for Social Security Benefits for Kathy and I. I certainly wasn't there, but I know what Mom told me. Grandma Bollan came down hard on Mom, telling them that Kathy and I hadn't seen Dad for years, that we weren't even his, and that

Mom didn't deserve a penny. None of this mattered in the end; we received benefits until we were eighteen. Grandma Bollan carried the pain and anger about losing her son with her to the end. She continued to blame AnnaBelle for everything until the day she passed away. Aunt Darlene, Dad's sister, would plead with her mother to understand that what happened to Otto was the result of how he chose to live his life, not the fault of AnnaBelle. Her plea's fell on Grandma's deaf ears, but I love her for trying.

After Dad's death, Kathy and I began to see a change in Stovall. I call him that now because I can. We were taught to call him "Dad" right after he married Mom. I never felt comfortable with it, probably because he was the farthest thing from a dad. The "touching" started almost immediately after Dad's death. As with all child molesters, there was always a threat if you told. I will not elaborate on this topic. I wish there were some way to stop these things from ever happening, every child deserves to have a happy, normal childhood. They should never be forced to endure something as degrading and embarrassing as these acts against them can be. I've often thought that once they were discovered, pedophiles' should perhaps carry a tattoo of a big "P" on their foreheads. Just for identification. It amazes me that they can scream about how unfair it is that they have to register as a sex offender, and not be able to live in a neighborhood like normal people after conviction. THEY ARE NOT NORMAL. They had a choice, their victims didn't. I'm drifting again.

Stovall also became a little more aggressive with our punishment, needing less than a good reason for it. We were not bad children, we knew better. He never went overboard with it unless Mom wasn't home. These became the times we feared. Again, there were the threats about telling Mom. She knew about the board with the holes in, but had no idea how often he used it. However, eventually she would find out.

Things went along as usual for a couple of years. Kathy and I still spent every moment we could at Grandma and Grandpa Wicker's house. We begged to go spend weekends, and would stay a week at a time in the summer when we could. It was "the" place to be. With four of our aunts and uncles being close to our own ages, they seemed like brothers and sisters to us. Mom's youngest sister, Janet, was one month younger than I was. It was great fun.

While I was in grade school, Grandma and Grandpa continued to live at Lowell. They lived in a small house on the outskirts of town, not too far from where AnnaBelle's Restaurant had been located. When I was about nine years old they made the move to Valparaiso, I was thrilled to have them so close, as was AnnaBelle. This time they moved to the perfect house, at least for all of us kids. It was a large house, located on the outskirts of Valpo. There was plenty of room to roam outside, and go on our adventures. The one thing that Grandma had a major problem with was the nudist colony across the road. Even though you would never have known it was there, Minnie knew it. I don't know how much land it encompassed, but it was all wooded. There was no way to see anything, except for the huge mansion located down the road and around the corner. Plus, it was all fenced. At the time I don't think I really understood, I just knew it was a bad place, and if you went inside the fence, you would never come out. But, being a kid, my memories are mainly of the fun we all had there.

It was about this same time that we were going to the Indiana Dunes every so often in the summer. Grandma and Mom would pack a huge lunch and we would all go spend the day. It was a great place, lots of things to do. I remember how cold the water was. It was amazing, it never warmed up. The sand was so hot it would burn your feet, but the water…. Like ice. We would try to run across the sand to get to the waters edge, sometimes I would stop and push my feet deep into the sand where it was cooler. You could almost hear a sizzle when your hot feet hit that cold water. We were never allowed to go back in the water right after we ate lunch. A lunch that consisted of half the sand I carried back with me. Does anyone else remember the sandy sandwiches eaten at beach outings?

During one of our summer trips to The Dunes, I somehow managed to get lost on the hiking trails after a "delicious" lunch of egg salad and sand. Since we all had to wait the required hour before going back to the beach, it was decided we would take a hike. (I'm sure our elders told us to take a hike.) Once we got on the trail, it split into two trails going in two different directions. So naturally the group split into two also. The girls went one way, the boys the other. We always traveled in a line, and the youngest was always in the rear. That was me, even though I wasn't really the youngest. I started with the girls, but then for some reason, decided to go back and follow my uncles. Well, naturally they were gone, I couldn't find them. So I turned around, went back to where the trails split and went to find the girls. I found that the trail began to split off at every turn. The woods had become quite dense, even though I called to them, no one heard me. I walked those trails for hours, I was terrified. Finally I saw a clearing, and headed for it. What I found at the edge of the clearing was a camp full of black people. At the time I was an eight year old little white girl from Valparaiso who had seen one family of blacks in my life. I was no longer terrified, there are no words to describe what I felt. I stood there looking at them, and they, in turn, stood looking at me. I'm sure they were just as shocked as I was. I was rooted for what seemed like forever. What to do? I thought about the dark woods, it was getting close to evening, I didn't want to go back there. I decided to take my chances and walked directly down the middle of that camp. My knees were shaking, I kept my eyes straight ahead, never looking anyone in the eye. The people that were outside just watched me walk by, I heard one kind lady ask if I was lost, I never replied. I made it to the road on the other side of the camp.... I lived. Our thoughts and beliefs were so ridiculous back in the 1950's. I know the people there wanted to help me, but I'm sure I scared them too.

I finally found the main highway and turned toward the water, I knew to do that much. As I approached the picnic area, there seemed to be a lot of commotion. There were police cars, a woman crying, people talking in groups, what was going on? I found out they were all looking for an eight year old girl that was missing. The crying woman was Mom. I can't remember the exact reaction when I walked up to them, but I do remember the look of relief in Moms eyes. Just to be back in her arms was all the comfort I needed. Thus ended my great adventure at the Indiana Dunes State Park. Good times.

Kathy and I never lacked for a nice home, food to eat, and nice clothes to wear, so I guess we were better off than a lot of kids back then. I am grateful for that, and Stovall never physically abused Mom. She was not yet the strong person she would become. Illness plagued her from an early age. Her appendix had to be removed when she was 16. Later, she developed a large tumor on her colon, forcing the doctors to remove a section. She had a hysterectomy before she was thirty. The one problem she could never overcome was the weakness of her respiratory system, caused by several bouts with pneumonia when she was a child living in Kentucky. Unfortunately, AnnaBelle would spend her life in and out of the hospital.

It was after her release from the hospital when we were 11 and 12 years old that suddenly brought on the infamous "mother, daughter talk". It was on a Saturday afternoon, we were cleaning the house and took a short break to rest. Since we had both become "young ladies", she felt it was the right time. Made even better because Stovall wasn't home, he had a Saturday route. The first thing she wanted to know was if anyone had ever touched us or done anything we knew they shouldn't have. It was all so embarrassing, but we finally told her the truth. She was furious. When he got home, it was not the happy home he had left that morning, but leave again he did. She ordered him out of the house.

She called the police, they picked him up and took him in for questioning. Then, Kathy and I were questioned by the police. It was a terrifying and embarrassing experience no child should have to endure. These were the very reasons kids were reluctant to tell. In the 1950's there were no rules about questioning children. Or should I say, if there was, the Valparaiso Police Department hadn't gotten the memo.

From there Mom and Stovall battled it out. He begged and pleaded, promised her a new life, a life somewhere else, anything, if only she would stay with him. He told her she could never make it raising Kathy and I alone, famous last words from most men back then. She weakened, and finally relented. I know the thought of perhaps having to depend upon her parents for help was the driving force behind her decision. They had already sacrificed so much for her and her two daughters. Stovall promised he would never touch either of us girls again. Mom didn't tell the family the truth about what had happened between them. I think it was just as well at the time.

Kathy and I did get to stay with Grandma and Grandpa while Mom and Stovall took a trip to St. Petersburg, Florida. He had acquaintances there, a couple named Carl and Marion Williams. A very nice couple that we would eventually call Uncle Carl and Aunt Marion. The trip had been an excursion to check out the area for jobs, housing, and schools. Stovall stayed true to his word, he moved Mom to a new city, and started a new life.

It was in September of 1959 when we packed all of our belongings and took off for St. Petersburg. I wasn't happy, I missed my Grandparents, aunts, and uncles, before we left the city limits of Valparaiso. But Mom was happy, and at this point, that was the most important thing. Her love for change and new places had already taken us to various places to live. This would be the beginning of the journey that drew Mom, Kathy and I even closer, due in part to our isolation from the rest of the family. But I think mainly because that's all there really was, just the three of us. No one could ever break through that bond......not ever.

Grandpa and Grandma Bollan   (William and Effie)
At Dad's Grave (Otto)   1956

Carolyn Sue   1960   St. Petersburg
Meadowlawn Jr. High School

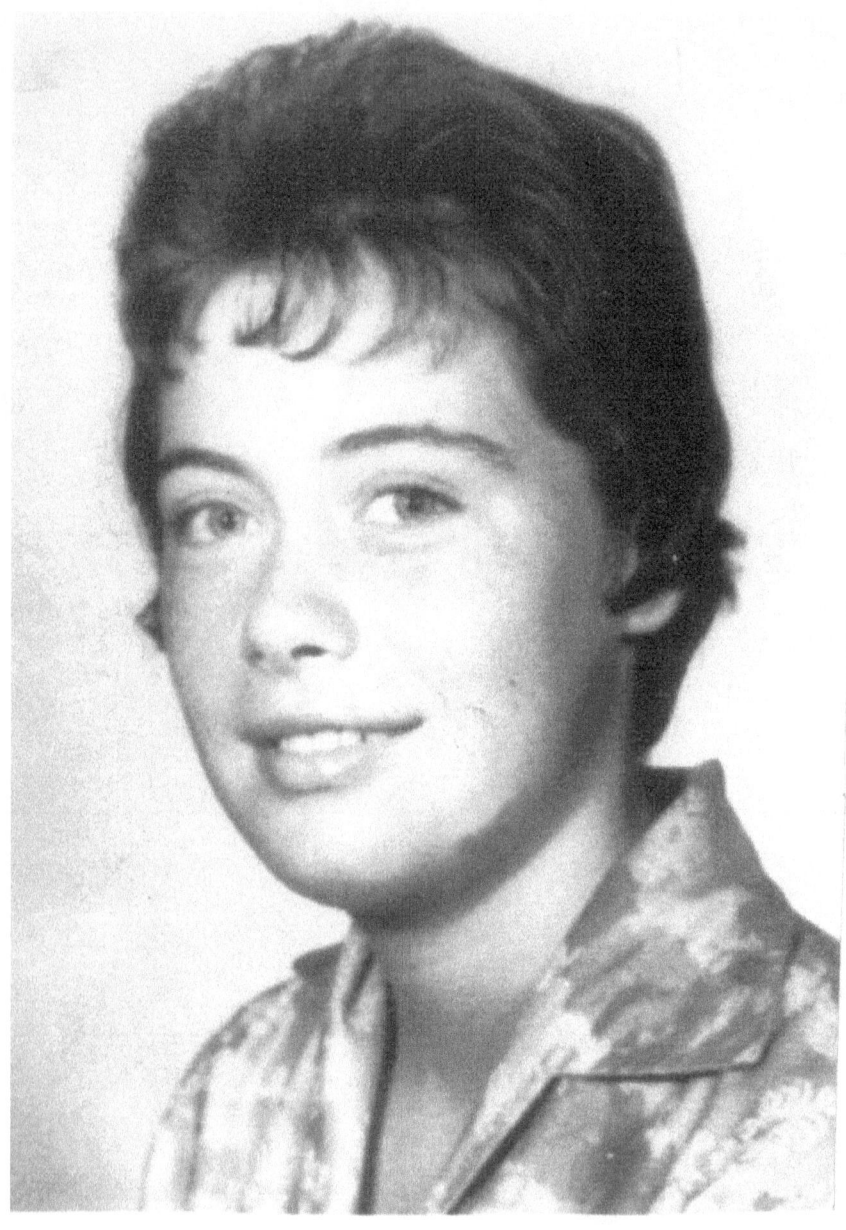

Kathy   1960   St Petersburg
Meadowlawn Jr. High School

Chapter V

A New Life Starts In St. Petersburg

Life in St Petersburg agreed with AnnaBelle from the very beginning. She loved the sunshine, the beaches, and the endless supply of fresh oranges and grapefruit. Her health improved, and for the most part there was peace at home. They had rented a small two bedroom apartment on the northwest side of the city; it was close to Carl and Marion. Stovall had put his application in at the Coke-a-Cola Company while he and Mom were there for their first visit. His job was waiting for him when we arrived. It wasn't a far stretch from what he had done in Valparaiso; he worked for Seyferts Potato Chips. Both were route jobs, both paid well with good benefits.

Kathy and I started school right away, it was the middle of September and school was already in session. As was the heat, it was so hot. Unfortunately, I had been exposed to mumps before we left Columbia School in Valpo and no one knew it at the time. I attended one day at Glenoak Elementary School and woke up the next morning with my jaw swollen, and painful. Mom called the school, they called Valparaiso, and by that afternoon we discovered where they came from. I had unwittingly exposed the entire sixth grade to the mumps, not one of my better days.

Before the end of that school year we moved to a larger apartment, I liked it better, there were a lot of windows, and it was bright and cheery. By the end of June, Mom and Stovall had bought a house at 753 41st Avenue N.E., located in a new subdivision about three blocks from Tampa Bay. In July the construction was completed and we moved to our new home. It was the one and only time in her life that AnnaBelle would totally own the home that she lived in.

Kathy and I took to the neighborhood right away. There were lots of kids. It never takes long for children to find each other, we were no exception. Directly in back of our house, across the *alley, lived the Gieger's, Mike, Chuck, and Nancy. Their mothers name was Mary; their Dad had passed away a few years earlier. Of course, Kathy and I thought that would be wonderful, not to have to put up with a dad in your life. Down the block on the corner lived the Bible family, Dick and June, (no, not Dick and Jane) their kids were Ricky and Debbie. Though younger than the rest of us, they were great kids and a lot of fun. Their parents had one employee at home, a maid and nanny combination, her name was Cornelius, we all loved her. She tolerated our constant jokes and mischief. Then there was Mark and Kim Butson in the next block and Linda Quimby, down the block from them. She would end up being a friend for life. We all became very close over the next couple of years; they soon learned to dislike Stovall almost as much as we did. You can't fool children for long. "You can fool some of the people all of the time, and all of the people some of the time, but you'll never fool all of the people all of the time".*

Kathy and I started school that September at Meadowlawn Jr. High School, located in northeast St. Petersburg. We were among the first students to attend the new school. It was a beautiful school, but hot, so very hot. There was no air conditioning at the time. September is still a sultry month in the south.

It was about this same time that the Wicker family moved from Valparaiso, Indiana to McArthur, Ohio. Grandpa decided to open an auction house. They did have relation living there too. Grandma's brother Jerry Griffith had lived there for years with his wife and family. It was a small town south of Columbus, not far from Athens. A very small town, Grandma called it the wasteland of the world. I don't think she was too happy there. But Edgil, like his daughter AnnaBelle, loved new places and a new adventure. They were both willing to take chances.

AnnaBelle was in heaven with her new home. She started work at the W.T. Grant Co., a newly opened store in the Northeast Shopping Center, not far from our house. She loved her job and all the people she met. This was where she met Don Amechi and his wife; they shopped there often, mostly for linens. They always asked for her, and she was happy to help them, he had a good sense of humor, teasing Mom incessantly. Almost everyone liked Mom, she was beautiful, and had a brilliant smile.

For the next two years, life passed without too many conflicts. Stovall stayed true to his word and never sexually touched us again. He did, however, use the infamous board with the holes in it as often as possible. It was never when Mom was home, therefore she wasn't even aware of it. She knew it was there, she knew he threatened with it, but not that he used it. Once again, you don't tell. I think we all know that if you can just hang in there long enough, something is bound to change.

That change eventually came. Mom had been in the hospital for a bleeding ulcer, imagine that. She had spent four very long days away from us; it was not a good time. Living with a crazy person doesn't allow you to sleep or rest well. There's always that little built in alarm ready to go off. He used the board once while she was gone, but that was once too many. I realize people may find it hard to believe, but there was never a time that we deserved the punishment he doled out. Kathy sassed once in a while, but not to that extent, we knew better. I would bend over backward to keep peace in that house, I hated conflict. The only ones that knew our fate were the kids that had become our confidants. On with the story.

It was during this time that Mom scheduled the dreaded "swimming lessons" for Kathy and I. She had decided that her daughters would not go through life with the same fear of water that kept her sitting on the beach instead of enjoying the water. When Mom was a child growing up in Kentucky, there were rope bridges (swinging bridges) spanning most of the creeks that could quickly rise in the spring of the year. She had never liked the bridges, but she was forced to use them at times when the water was too high to cross on foot. It was the only way to get home from school. One day, while crossing one of these bridges, her brother Ray decided to start swinging the bridge when she was about half way across. He was always joking around and doing something he shouldn't have, this was no exception. Or just maybe, it was re-payment for that rock he took to the back of his head, thanks to his sister, AnnaBelle. At any rate, the creek was high with rapidly moving water. Needless to say, she lost her footing and fell in. She almost drowned before Grandpa could pull her out. With the grace of God, he happened to be close by on his way home from work.

Mom's near drowning experience was the reason for our swimming lessons. At that point, I swear, I could have personally flown to Indiana and threw rocks at Uncle Ray myself, what was he thinking??? Mom enrolled the two of us in summer classes at the Spa Pool, located at the southern tip of St Pete, by the Municipal Pier. What with my fear of water, this was the worst thing possible ...ever. Mom decided that her daughters would not go through life without the ability to swim. Actually, this made sense, living in Florida, surrounded by water. But then I ask you, what's wrong with an inner-tube?

Mom was admitted to the hospital the night before our first swimming lesson. She had hired a woman to come in during the day to take care of the house, and watch over the two of us. The first two days I told the woman I couldn't go to the lessons because it was "my time of the month". Then she told Mom about it. Well, Mom knew my "time" had came and gone the week before. She let me know in no uncertain terms that my "time" was up, I had to go. Naturally, Kathy took to the water like a fish, making me look even worse. Our instructors name was Moe, he was pretty patient with me, at first. All he asked me to do the first day was jump in the pool. I knew I would drown, the water looked bottomless, I refused, and refused, and refused. He finally said either I had to jump or go over to the kiddy pool with the little ones. As tempted as I was to go, looking at the four year olds was a deal breaker. I told him I would jump, but my inevitable death would be on his conscience. I closed my eyes and took the plunge, waiting for my final gasps for air as I sank to the depths of this godforsaken hellhole. Surprisingly, when I realized I was still breathing, I opened my eyes to find I was standing in four feet of water. Before the day was over, I discovered he was telling the truth, I would come back to the top if I held my breath. I was jumping off at the twelve foot mark by the time I left that day. We spent two months taking lessons and

I loved every day of it. Well, until I did a jackknife off the diving board and Moe had to save me. That time, I didn't rise to the top. In the end, we both passed our swimming tests, and found that, once again, Mom was right.

When Mom came home from the hospital we were so relieved. Things had been a little rough with Step Dad while she was gone. On the day of her return, I was changing the sheets on her bed while she was in the bathroom. She returned while I was still bent over tucking in the sheets. She saw the bruises on the back of my legs, with the distinguishing hole marks. She flew into a rage at the sight. Stovall was at work that day, I begged her to calm down before he came home. Kathy and I were both sorry we had not told her sooner, she had a right to know. She went to the kitchen and got a butcher knife to put under her pillow. Again, with the butcher knife. She was in no condition to be fighting with anyone, so we decided to bide our time. It would be the last time he would use the board on anyone. It was the beginning of the end for Stovall.

Things finally came to a head about two months later on a Saturday evening, the night before Mother's Day. I had celebrated my fourteenth birthday the month before. It was 1961. Mom had taken Kathy and I shopping for dresses for our first school dance. Stovall never liked us going anywhere without him. Looking back now, I know it was a control issue with him. He made sure Kathy and I were seldom alone with Mom. I imagine he was worried about what we might tell her. In hindsight, I wish we would have told her sooner, it was his fear factor that kept us quiet. I never thought for a moment she would leave him, he constantly reminder her that she couldn't make it without him. He was proven wrong, so very wrong.

By the time we returned home from our shopping trip, it was getting late. The regular time for supper had passed; it was around 7 P.M. Stovall started complaining as soon as we walked through the door. Then the questions started. Where did we go, what did we do, how long were we there, who did we see? Finally, Mom had all she could take. She told him she was starting supper. He said he already ate, and for some unknown reason, Kathy and I had to go to bed without supper. Well, that did it, Mom blew up. She said there was no way we were going to bed without our supper.

The more their anger grew, the louder their voices became, until they were yelling at each other. Mom took a can of soup out of the cabinet, opened it, poured it in a pan, and went to the stove to heat it up. Then he flew into a rage. He went out the backdoor into the garage and pulled the main electrical fuses. The stove was electric. As he came back through the door Mom grabbed a box of Cheerios and started pouring them into cereal bowls. She was shaking so hard she could barely hit the bowls. By now the yelling had escalated to screaming, cussing and name calling. Mom's favorite name for him turned out to be "bastard", and he in turn, seemed to think she was a "whore" a "bitch", and something called a "rip" (for some unknown reason, this was the name I learned to hate, just as much as the man that used it, "daddy dearest").

Mom finally said the magic words, "she wasn't going to put up with him anymore, and he would never lay a hand on her daughters again". In two long strides, he was across the kitchen and swept the cereal, bowls, milk and spoons off the countertop. There were Cheerios everywhere, the floor was a mess. As he raised his hand to strike Mom, Kathy stepped in and grabbed it. All I seemed to be able to do was cry; this was bad, very, very bad.

He somehow grabbed Kathy and got her out the backdoor and into the garage. The next thing I knew he had her bent backward over the trunk of his car, choking her. Mom jumped on his back, trying to pull him off Kathy. All I could do was stand at the outside garage door and scream for help. Mom began to hit him as hard as she could, but it seemed he felt nothing, by this time he had went berserk. That was a new word of the day for me.

During this entire episode, the garage door was wide open. In our neighborhood the houses were close together, I know the neighbors could hear my pleas for help, but no one came. Maybe they, too, were terrified of this crazy man. After all, it was almost dark by now, and there were no lights illuminating the garage, or the nightmare that was unfolding inside.

I ran back to Mom, trying to help, by now Kathy was turning blue. Even the two of us together could not stop him. It was then that what can only be called a miracle took place, the door bell rang. Stovall let go of Kathy and stood up straight, shoving Mom and I out of the way. He then turned and walked back through the kitchen to answer the front door. Mom grabbed Kathy and together we pulled her outside the garage, we had to get away before he came back. Kathy somehow found the strength to run, and run we did.

It was two blocks to Linda Quimby's house, that's where we stopped running. We went to door and started knocking. Linda's father opened the door to find three crying females. Her parents knew Kathy and me both, but had never met Mom. They welcomed us into their home and called the police. Luckily, Linda's mother was a nurse, she quickly checked Kathy over while we waited on the police. The Quimby's were the nicest, kindest people we had met in Florida, I will forever be grateful to them for coming to our aid.

When the police arrived, they started writing down the report of what had happened. The three of us were still shaking; the tremors just would not stop. We were a mess. As God is my witness, I have never hated another human being as much as I hated Jim Stovall. Hate is not a word I use lightly, but as far as I was concerned, he should be dead. All the years of fear and dread seemed to be focused on this one night. Everyone will reach a point where they have reached their limit, all three of us had reached ours. We never wanted to see him again. The fear had now risen to terror.

After about an hour, it took that long to stop the crying and shaking, the police decided to take us back to the house to gather a few belongings. They would not leave us there, not for another moment. I think all three of us were still a little dazed, to say the least. In the end, AnnaBelle was right, she was done putting up with him, and his abuse. We finally followed the officers to their car and got in the back seat. It was time to go home and face the music, or should I say the maniac.

When we pulled up in front of the house, Kathy nor I either one wanted to go in. The officers assured us that "stepdad" wouldn't touch us. We had to pack some clothes and personal items; they were going to take us to a motel. You would not have believed the scene when we walked through the front door and into the living room. Stovall sat there watching television, as though nothing had happened. I didn't care, I went to pack.

While the three of us were gathering our things, we could hear the police questioning him; he denied the entire incident ever happened. As I said, he was crazy. The officer named Phil accused him of choking Kathy, he denied it again. Phil called him a SOB, and told him there were bruises around the neck of his daughter. That would be the last time anyone called us his daughters. (This fact alone made the entire situation somehow worthwhile.) He was telling them that he was just watching television when the doorbell rang and he answered it. It was the jeweler that had repaired his watch. He was on his way home and decided our house was close enough that he would just drop the watch off. We never knew exactly who the jeweler was, all we knew was that he was our angel of mercy.

The officers took Mom, Kathy, and I to a motel on the other side of the city after we left the house. They wanted to make sure Stovall couldn't find us. They were kind enough to stop and buy sandwiches for us to take to the motel, we still hadn't eaten supper. They were apologetic about not being able to take him into custody that night. It seems that because it was a holiday weekend, they couldn't get a bench warrant for his arrest until Monday morning. It didn't matter, we knew we were safe. They patrolled around the motel most of the night to make sure he didn't show up. They even assigned an officer to watch the house in case he tried to leave it to find us.

After they finally left the three of us alone in our room, we took showers, put on our pajama's, and ate supper. It was well after midnight by the time we laid down to try and get some sleep. Even in our exhaustion we continued to talk until almost dawn. We slept late, waking up to a beautiful, happy Mother's Day.

By the time the warrant was issued for his arrest on Monday morning he was gone. The neighbors watched him pack his car full of everything he could on Sunday. Sometime during the night, the officers that were watching the house followed him when he drove off, just to make sure he didn't go to the motel. They followed him north to the city limits, unable to do anything without the needed warrant. I have to ask myself what they would have done if Kathy had been horribly injured or killed. Wait until Monday? What a travesty that was, he got away with it. The charges were TBH. Threatening Bodily Harm. Threatening????

For the sake of safety, they kept us at the motel for three more days. Kathy and I didn't care, it was wonderful not to have to wake up in the mornings and see Stovall. Mom, on the hand, wanted to go home and check on her things. It would have to wait.

We returned to the house on Wednesday, only to find he had taken more that Mom had thought. The only linens left in the house were on the beds, and he left three towels and washrags. Once again, he was a "bastard", and he really was for taking all the things Mom had worked so hard to buy. But then, how much could it really matter? He was gone.

We spent our first free night at home sitting at the dining room table going through photographs. Every photo we found with Stovall in it was laid aside until we had finished going through everything. Then all three of us got a pair of scissors and began cutting him out of each and every picture. Mom brought an ashtray and lighter to the party so we burned every image of him out of the house. It was like an exorcism. Only we did what a priest couldn't, we rid ourselves of him completely and forever.

The officer named Phil Pecora took us under his wing. He changed the locks on all the doors, and made sure the house was safe. They also continued to patrol through the neighborhood for weeks, just to be sure he didn't return. The department had pursued his arrest; they contacted his family in Indiana, and watched for him in the area. They never found him, they never would. Did they honestly expect his parents to say "Yes, he's right here at our house in Boswell, come on up and arrest him"?

The most important thing that came about, happened in that motel room Mother's Day morning. For the first time in her life, AnnaBelle took complete control of not only her life, but the lives of her daughters. She knew that day there would never again be a time that a man would tell her what to do, or hurt one of her children. She stayed true to this vow for the rest of her life.

Chapter VI

LOSE ONE STOVALL.... GAIN A BETTER LIFE

Annabelle quit her job at W. T. Grant Company, shortly after Stovall left. She went to work in downtown St. Pete, at a cocktail lounge located in one of the hotels near the piers. It was a beautiful place. She made good money, something she needed now that she was a single mother. She loved her new freedom, she loved the fact that Kathy and I could live without fear, and she loved the happiness that now controlled our lives. The house that once was so cold and full of fear had now become a warm and content home for the three of us. We were in heaven.

Kathy and I were out of school for the summer. Most of our time was spent having fun. We went to St. Pete Beach, had picnics with the neighborhood kids, and went to the show every Saturday afternoon. Our constant companion was Linda Quimby. She was an only child, so Kathy and I were her new sisters. It was fine with us, we loved her dearly. The three of us went to see every new movie that hit the theater, from "On The Beach" with Gregory Peck to "Wild In The Country" with Elvis. "The Birds", by Alfred Hitchcock left us terrified of flying things for months, but I thought Susanne Pleshette was beautiful. Edgar Allan Poe's "The House Of Usher" left a permanent mark on me, I was fascinated by him. But, best of all were our beloved musicals, especially "South Pacific", and the soundtrack that we just had to have. "I'm Gonna Wash That Man Right Out Of My Hair", was one power I would have loved to have had later in life. The song that set my young dreams spinning was "Some Enchanted Evening", I knew that would be my experience some day. (It was an experience all right.) Anyway, we did love our new found freedom.

As summer wore on Kathy and I started to talk more about seeing Grandma and Grandpa and our aunts and uncles that we loved so much. Mom felt bad because she neither drove, nor had the extra money to buy tickets for us to take the trip up north. Then a couple she had become acquainted with had decided to take a vacation to Canada, and would be going through Ohio. They agreed to take the two of us with them, and drop us off in McArthur. This was the answer to our prayers. Although Mom didn't want us to go, she knew it was for the best. We would stay three weeks, by then, she would save the money to fly up and then bring us home with her.

As it turned out, it was good for Mom to have some time to herself. She had never been completely alone; there had always been someone, or something to care for. She enjoyed her time of freedom. AnnaBelle would become good friends with the officer named Phil Pecora, and even date him for a short time. They both finally agreed that they made betters friends than lovers, and remained that way for years. They did make a beautiful couple; they both had black curly hair and gorgeous blue eyes.

Time passed quickly after we left on our trip north. Before Mom knew it, it was time for her to fly to Ohio, see her parents, and bring Kathy and I back home. Mom found that she was as excited as we had been at the prospect of getting away for a few days. I had gotten into a huge patch of poison ivy while clearing an outdoor cement staircase for Grandma. Did I know about the three leaf rule? Never heard of it. It spread over my entire body. Grandma tried everything she knew to help it, even down to a soda bath, calamine lotion, and a trip to the doctor's office. Since I told them I didn't want a shot, he gave me pills, needless to say they didn't work. It was the dog days of a very hot August. I was miserable, sleeping on the floor at night in the dining room. The cool linoleum floor felt wonderful. I was a mess by the time Mom arrived.

The very first morning after Mom got there she took me back to the doctor. Just like any other mother, she didn't care if I "wanted" a shot or not, I got one. She was right, within a day, the dreaded poison ivy was beginning to dry up.

Just as Kathy and I had enjoyed our time with our Grandparents, Mom was thrilled to be able to spend some much needed time with her parents. All in all, except for the poison ivy issue, we had a wonderful visit. The following weekend, Grandpa took the three of us to the Columbus Airport, and we flew home. I had missed Mom more than I thought possible. It was good to have things back to normal. Normal had quickly become just the three of us. We had so many things to catch up on. When the plane landed in Tampa, Mr. and Mrs. Quimby were waiting on us, with our best friend, Linda. I think she missed us as much as we missed her.

Soon it was September, and the start of a new school year. I returned for my third year at Meadowlawn Jr. High, starting my freshman year. Kathy started her sophomore at the high school next door. We both felt as though a lifetime had passed since we last saw our schoolmates. Even I knew how much better we seemed to the teachers that knew us last year. We were happy, and it showed in our attitude.

AnnaBelle continued her work at the lounge, meeting new people and making good friends. Times were a little tougher due to finances, but it didn't matter, we were thankful for what we didn't have….. Stovall. We found the peace of mind alone made the sacrifices well worth it. Because Mom was still receiving social security, we managed to live comfortably. At fourteen and fifteen, we were happy, healthy girls. Even Mom's health had improved to the point she seldom saw her doctors. Obviously, the biggest source of her illness was gone.

From the time I first met him, I had a crush on Mark Butson, he was my first serious crush. Yes, there was my love for Bobby Eustis in the third grade, but that memory faded when I met this challenge. Everyone knew it, including Mark. He was older than me by one year, and more than a little arrogant, but I found out later that most of the arrogance was an act. I received my first kiss from Mark when I was thirteen. It happened at his fourteenth birthday party. It was a kiss that went beyond a friendly little birthday kiss. He was receiving a kiss from each girl there (as I said, arrogant). When he kissed me, it seemed to go on forever. I was certainly in no mind to push him away. His mother finally did it for me, she pulled him away. She was also a single mother; she was raising two sons by herself, never an easy task.

As the school year progressed, Kathy and I started talking to Mom about moving back up north. We missed everyone in the family so much, and so did Mom. She finally relented and began to check into making arrangements. Maybe it was time for us to have a change of scenery. Nothing excited AnnaBelle like planning for a move and then following through with it. We both knew this, so convincing her turned out to be an easy task. The planning and attention to details was what seemed to take the longest. But surprisingly, Mom had our new life ready to embark upon within two months.

Kathy and I would, once again, go to live with Grandma and Grandpa in Ohio. There, we would attend school for the rest of that year. We could not have been any happier; I had no clue about the extra burden this would put on Grandma, she still had three children at home to clean, cook, and do laundry for. Her burdens in life were many. I can only hope we didn't add to them too much.

AnnaBelle would start a career, to ensure that she could care for, and support her daughters. This would be the longest they had ever been separated, it was the least of the girl's worries, and the biggest dread for their Mother. Packing was a chore, everything had to go. She would never give up her dishes, silver, or pots and pans, so AnnaBelle knew these would have to be packed for storage until the time that they found a permanent home. Selling the furniture wasn't an easy task, but selling her beloved home was heartbreaking for her.

When all the packing, selling, and shipping was over, the only things left were the suitcases full of the clothing and personal belongings that we absolutely had to have. We spent our final night in St. Petersburg at a motel, leaving for the airport early the next morning. We were taken to the Tampa Airport by none other than Mr. & Mrs. Quimby, along with their extremely unhappy daughter, Linda. We knew Linda was going to miss us as much as we would her. Little did she know the extent of our love for her. She was the second real friend I had ever had. I wouldn't have another for many years, ironically her name too, would be Linda. Saying goodbye at the gate was heartbreaking, we had to leave a sobbing Linda behind. In the end, we cried as hard as she did. Boarding the plane, we knew we were not going to return, even though we all three vowed we would see each other soon. We would keep that promise, but it wasn't soon, it was nearly thirty-five years later.

Mom, Kathy, and I flew into the airport at Columbus, Ohio on a cold November day. We were expecting Uncle Bud and Aunt Darlene to be there to greet us. The two of them had traveled from Missouri for a visit, and to see their sister and nieces. They were supposed to be there to pick us up and transport us to Grandma and Grandpa's at McArthur. As soon as we entered the airport we heard a page for AnnaBelle Stovall (yes, she still had that God awful name), she needed to report to the nearest service desk. It was Uncle Bud, he and Aunt Darlene had been in an automobile accident in Columbus, and were being treated at the hospital. We immediately retrieved our luggage and took a taxi to the hospital. Our aunt and uncle were both injured, but they would be released as soon as Grandpa arrived to pick us all up. He drove one car and our Uncle Jerry drove another to Columbus. There was no possible way to get everyone and all the suitcases in one vehicle. Sadly, Uncle Bud's car was a total loss.

It was a long drive back home that evening, but everyone was thankful that the accident wasn't any worse, and the injuries would heal quickly. It could have been a scary omen, but no one paid it any mind. Being back with our loved ones was all that really mattered to Kathy and I, not to mention being able to attend school with our aunt and uncles. Mom was excited about her new future also, made even better because her plans were falling into place.

Since AnnaBelle had always wanted to be a beautician, it seemed logical to head in that direction. She had two aunts that were directors at The House Of James Beauty Colleges in Indiana. One was located in Jeffersonville, Indiana, the other in South Bend, with the main headquarters at Indianapolis. The schools were elaborate, as were the beauty shops that carried the same name. Mr. James would have it no other way. He toured the facilities often for inspections; everyone felt his wrath if things were found to be less than the standards he had set. Aunt Gertrude was in South Bend, but AnnaBelle chose to go to Jeffersonville. This was where her Aunt Katie ruled over the school with a tight reign. The dorm was located above the school, and housed up to ten students. Aunt Katie lived in a large, gracious home located across the street from the Ohio River. It was a beautiful place, built in Victorian style. It was also owned by Mr. James. It was here that AnnaBelle would live, along with her Aunt Katie and Katie's only child, Kenneth. She started beauty college in November, while her daughters had started their school year at McArthur. Everything seemed to be falling into place.

AnnaBelle found she was finally within her elements; she loved attending school, and loved the idea of finally having the career she had only dreamed of. The only thing that marred her happiness was missing her daughter's, and knowing the extra burden she had again put upon her parents. She did go back to McArthur for Christmas, taking her daughters a puppy, and her Mother a beautiful set of china. The china was welcome, the puppy, maybe not so much. The kids all loved the little black furry ball, but her mother could have lived without it. A friend of the kids, Richard, named the puppy Say-So, no one knew why. You would Say it fit her, So you see, it stuck.

AnnaBelle was in Jeffersonville about three months when her friend, Phil Pecora, quit his job as a police officer in St. Petersburg and joined her in Indiana. He enrolled at the House Of James and started his own career. She was glad to see him, they remained friends for years. He achieved something rare for a man in the 1960's; he became a well established hair dresser. Women loved him, he was handsome, and he was popular.

Annabelle began to have health issues again at the beginning of the year, shortly after her trip home for Christmas. Living so close to the Ohio River was taking a toll on her respiratory system. This led to other problems, due to her weak immune system. She ended up *having emergency surgery for her colon; they had to remove a tumor and a section. All her family in Ohio could do that day was pray. She made it through the procedure, but, recovery took some time. She couldn't attend classes for two months, her grades suffered. There were times when she wondered if it was all worth it, but in her heart, she knew she had to continue.*

The beginning of June found Mom waiting for the arrival of Kathy and I. School was out for the summer, we were once again joining our Mother. Mom had rented a small apartment for the three of us. She was trying to work part time, and go to school, never an easy task. We were 15 & 16 now, not too much trouble. We spent some of our time with our cousin, Kenny. Most of the time was used to explore Jeffersonville. All three of us had allies at the college; someone was always willing to take us off for the day. We spent time across the river at Louisville; there were parks and fun activities to be found there. We were always in good hands. Summer passed quickly.

We started school that year at Jeffersonville High School. It was not one of my favorite schools, the halls and classrooms were dark, not very appealing. As usual though, our lives were ever changing, this year would be no exception. By the end of October, we moved to Indianapolis.

AnnaBelle could not catch up in her studies, Mr. James saw this, and the two daughters she was responsible for. He decided to pull her out of college and make her manager of his beauty shop located in Broadripple, at Indy. She was classy, beautiful, and a definite asset to his business, he didn't want to lose her. This move was fine with Kathy and I, we were more than ready to put Jeffersonville behind us. It was always fun to see what was waiting at our next location.

Chapter VII

On To Indianapolis

AnnaBelle's Spirit Breaks Free

The move to Indianapolis was a good idea. Leaving Jeffersonville caused no remorse what-so-ever for any of us. We never cared for the town, nor did we have any close ties there, except for Aunt Katie and our cousin Kenny. Mom rented a two bedroom apartment located at 6126 Compton Street in Broadripple. It was in a nice area and across the street from the high school we would attend. We were enrolled at Broadripple High School shortly after we arrived. Kathy was in her Junior year, I was a Sophomore. Again, we found ourselves in a school that felt foreign to both of us. It was not a friendly school, therefore it wasn't long until I would dread everyday that I had to walk through the front door.

The beauty shop where AnnaBelle would start as manager was a beautiful place. Elegant would be a good word to describe it. The women that worked there were very happy with their new boss, she fit in quite well. Kathy and I never lacked for hair styles, or the latest "dos". Someone was always doing our hair. We spent many hours at the shop after school, waiting for Mom to close so we could all go home. It was a fun place to hang out. We would help out with cleaning at times, the beauticians were good to us.

I remember at Christmas that year Mom bought Kathy and I each a new winter coat, they were knee length. She gave them to us at the shop that was where they had been delivered, they were beautiful. Kathy's was camel hair, tan in color, and had a large fur collar; it was very popular item at that time. Mine was darker with an A-line cut, and also had a large fur collar. Then, two days before Christmas, Sears delivered a new console. It was a television, radio, and stereo system combination. I will never forget that day, we were thrilled. We hadn't had a TV for months, but more than that, it included a record player. It was a Curtis Mathis product.

I soon became bored with school, I applied for a job at the local drive-in restaurant, Borky's Drive-In. Although I was only fifteen, they hired me. Because I told the owner I was sixteen. All was well until I celebrated my sixteenth birthday. My boss wasn't happy about it, but he kept me. I was so grateful.

The job turned out to be a learning experience; being a shy teenager, it helped me learn to deal with people. It was a busy place, very popular for their excellent food. I worked outside as a "curb girl". I have to tell you there were some characters working there. First came the identical twins, Dottie and Doris. They had worked there for years. Both were very outgoing and very out-spoken, I would learn many things from these two women. It wasn't always information a sixteen year old needed to know. Actually, it was information that no one needed to know, at any age. It seemed their biggest joy in life came from causing me great embarrassment. I guess it was worth it, they actually liked me. I soon learned they didn't like very many people. They gave me tips on how to dress for work. Our uniforms consisted of white blouses, with "Borky's" in red letters on the back, and our name embroidered on the front. Then, there were the required "snug" black slacks. "You always have to wear a girdle", the twins told me. Again, I thought they were joking, until they had our boss, Bob, tell me. That was really embarrassing. For once I should have believed them. But on the up side, they were the best waitresses at Borky's, and gave me the best training. Later on, I would end up training the new hires on the four to midnight shifts.

There were others there that remain in my mind. There was the night manager, Larry. I developed a crush, or something, for him. It had to be because he was older. It certainly wasn't his personality .....what was I thinking? What a low life he was. Then there was the soda guy, Will (not his real name....please read the following obvious reasons why). His girlfriend wouldn't have sex with him, but she would pose for nude pictures that her dad took, and then give them to him. She would have been the ultimate tease, and her *dad the ultimate pervert. I spent a month with her one day when Larry and Will took her and I to Brown County for an outing. It quickly became the day from hell. Crush or no crush, this guy was an idiot. He wanted to take a ride on a bicycle built for two. Sounds like fun, doesn't it? It may have been, with anyone but Larry. He scared the living crap out of me on the hills and paths around the park. I'm sure there was a race somewhere that day, he must have thought he was in it. When he finally brought the instrument of death to a stop, I felt like doing the thing where you jump off, throw yourself down, kiss the ground, and cry "land, beautiful land".*

Larry and I spent the entire day trying to avoid eye contact with the weird girlfriend . We were duly sworn to secrecy about the nude problem. The only thing I got out of the day was a little wooden keepsake box with Brown County painted on it. Oh, and good reason to lose the crush on Larry. During the very, very, long trip home, I quickly decided Will and I were the only sane ones in the car. That wasn't saying a lot, look at what we were dating.

As it ended up, I really wasn't losing too much. I was pretty sure Larry had a "thing" for Mom. He was constantly telling me that I had a pretty face, but I needed to lose weight. This from a guy that weighed about 300 pounds at one time. Again, what was I thinking? One of my fondest memories was the night he thought he could teach Mom to drive. His new Grand Prix was the only real love of his life. He was visibly shaken by the time she got done with his car, and still couldn't tell the gas pedal from the brake. Good times.

I soon learned about the "salad lady", Mae. She was a large black woman. I don't think I ever saw her on her feet, she sat at a table and made salads. Seriously, I never once saw her get up and walk around. Larry told me about her past; it seems she had operated a "house of ill repute". I didn't believe him until she started telling me about her "special house, and her special girls". She planned on opening another place in New Orleans, just as soon as the police forgot about the first one. She asked me to come to work for her. I was pretty sure I wouldn't be waiting on tables, maybe working the curb, someone's curb…… somewhere. "Just say no" comes to mind.

I stayed at Borky's until we moved again. It was probably none too soon, I think I started to become one of "them". Even the boss became stranger by the day. Someone had told him that drinking milk after consuming a half pint of vodka would disguise the smell. They were so wrong.

Although AnnaBelle loved her job, she felt restless. Money was still an issue, it wasn't easy raising teenagers. As she became acquainted with more people in Indianapolis, she began to socialize. There was a new club close to downtown Indy called The Purple Tree Lounge, she would go there with her friends. Of course she stood out in the crowd; she was more stunning than ever. Eventually the owner asked if she would be interested in working for him, she was. She had heard rumors that Mr. James was going to close the shop; it seemed like the right time to make a change. She accepted the job at the Purple Tree Lounge.

Mom dated a few times, but never anything serious. There was one guy named Jack, their friendship kept them close, but nothing more. When he would come to pick Mom up, she was never ready, so he would spend time talking to Kathy and I. Mom had told us he was an agent, I don't remember if it was the FBI or the CIA. He told us that the only thing a boy wanted from us at our age was to "get in our pants", and not to believe a word they told us. It would be lies, all lies, they had only one motive, to "get in our pants". I was in a constant state of embarrassment when he was present, even though he was seriously trying to give us some sound advice. At the time Johnny Mathis was the rage, at least to me. I loved his music, and bought every new album he released. Jack told me he was at a party in Hollywood the year before, while there, he had met my Johnny Mathis. I wanted information, he gave me way to much. He said, "Mathis is as queer as a three dollar bill". His words, not mine. I just knew he was lying, teasing again, and I let it slide. That was in 1962, it would be in the 1990's before I realized he was telling the truth. But no matter, I still love Johnny Mathis, and I always will. His voice is beautiful, and his songs contain the essence of all the romance I dreamed of at that young age…… And, still do at times.

Unfortunately, about a year later, Jack was found shot to death in his apartment there in Indianapolis. He was a great guy, and a lot of fun. Evidently danger did follow him. He used to tell Mom people were following him, at these times he avoided seeing her, for her own safety. Kathy and I thought he was exaggerating, I guess he wasn't. He remains a good memory from my teenage years. And in the end, he was right, boys will tell you anything to "get in your pants". (I found a picture of Mom and Jack, I will include it at the end of this chapter.)

I have another memory of one of Mom's "boyfriends". This one had a car dealership there in Indy, they called him "Red". And yes, he had red hair. He really liked Mom. So much so that he would give Kathy and I cars to drive for a day or two at a time. Kathy always did the driving, she was pretty good. (It must have been those lessons Dad gave her when she was four years old.) We would cruise all over Broadripple. The best part, we never had to put gas in the car, he always left them with a full tank. One such car was a new Golden Commando Fury, a white convertible no less. A thing of beauty. Now I ask you, what kind of business man would give that kind of car to two teenaged, unlicensed, uninsured, untrained, girls. Well, I can tell you, it would be a man in lust. Yes, I said lust, he really had a thing for Mom. She, on the other hand, felt less than nothing for him, he was being to possessive, that wasn't working for AnnaBelle. Not to mention that she had told him not to give us any type of automobile to drive. What he thought would endear him to her, ending up biting him on the butt. Kathy and I begged and pleaded with her to date him a while longer. Lets face it, the cars were nice. She looked at us like we were from Mars, aliens, little alien children. We knew better than to drive the cars, and we knew Red was a done deal. We were right on both counts.

Some where along the line, AnnaBelle was offered a job working lunch and early afternoons at The Antelope Club, a private establishment for men. This was workable, she didn't report to the lounge until late afternoon. The Antelope Club was discussed at length in the first book. (I'm really trying not to be repetitive.) The pay here was exceptional, but soon the two jobs became a chore, and she had to choose between them. The choice was easy; it had to be the lounge. She bid the gentlemen at the Antelope Club farewell, and never looked back. They were, after all, a scary bunch. What with their hunting trips, guns, tall tales, and wild cuisine. They were however, wealthy men that paid their employee's generously. In return, they expected them to keep the club, and what happened there, private. Kind of like the Vegas slogan.

The Purple Tree was a beautiful, new, and trendy spot in town. It was part of the Manger Motor Inn and located closer to center of the city at Sixteenth Street and Illinois Avenue. This is where the stars would stay during their visits to the city. It was especially busy during the Indy 500. This was also where the social butterfly in AnnaBelle would emerge and find her wings; she enjoyed her life to the fullest. She came in contact with sports legends, singers, comedians, and the Indy drivers themselves. Andy Williams stood out as a nice person, Tommy Lasorda seemed a little arrogant to her.

The Purple Tree was also where she first encountered a very young, very under aged, David Letterman. As I stated in the first book, "The Journey, The Dreams, & AnnaBelle", he knew what he wanted as a teenager, and went after it. He needed to meet the stars, the people that would eventually become part of his career, and he did just that. Even though he was asked to leave on a regular basis (he was under age after all), she admired his tenacity. She enjoyed most everyone, with a few exceptions.

AnnaBelle was enjoying not only her job, but her life in general. She attended parties, went out to dinner, and spent time with her daughters. She loved the Indy 500, but, as with most people, enjoyed the time trials more. She loved the way the city came to life during the weeks prior to the event. She never missed the time trials, or the parties that followed. Every night was a new and exciting adventure for her. She was in her element here.

AnnaBelle soon found life a little easier, and the extra money made life better for all three of us. It wasn't long before she met the man that would eventually become the center of her world. There was just one big problem, he was married. This kind of behavior went against every fiber of her being. She had been the victim of "the other woman". Now, she herself was being tempted. His name was Joe Stoops; she was in love with him before she even realized it herself. He too, fell in love with her. It would take time, years even, but eventually he did get the necessary divorce. Though it slightly marred their relationship, they went forward with what would be the relationship of a lifetime. The two of them never married, it didn't seem like the right thing to do. It was probably just as well in the end.

In the meantime, AnnaBelle continued to meet various people with whom it was good to have ties. Joe was in sales, as were many of his friends. She would come in contact with lawyers, politicians, and the elite of the city. It wasn't long before a gentleman by the name of Pal Horton asked her to come to work for him. He owned a private club close to downtown Indy, appropriately named Pal's Lounge. This turned out to be an offer she couldn't refuse; he would pay her an outrageous amount of money. She was a very good cocktail waitress, an attractive cocktail waitress. Pal knew this, and knew she would be an asset to his business. It seemed to be a win, win situation for both of them.

In the meantime, I was still working at Borky's, but I had quit school, refusing to go. I had never liked Broadripple High School, that didn't change with time. Kathy would follow suit, Mom was beside herself with grief over the situation. There really wasn't much any mother could have done, we were both over sixteen, the legal age to quit. She had loved the idea that her daughters would have the opportunity she never had, to complete their education. Her dreams for us would eventually be realized; both of us would finish school, further our education, and hold good jobs in the future.

With her new job at Pal's Lounge, AnnaBelle found it necessary to move closer to downtown Indianapolis. It was too far to commute. In July, she rented a small apartment on the fourth floor of the Picadilly Apartment building, located on the corner of

Sixteenth Street and Pennsylvania Avenue. From here, she could walk the two short blocks to work each afternoon. She worked from four to closing, which varied with the cliental. Sometimes she would get home around 2AM; sometimes it would be closer to 3. Because it was a private club they didn't open until four in the afternoon, even though the city didn't really come to life until nine or ten at night. It was a small place, and the members were among the upper crust of Indy. These were people you would want to know in time of need, any need. Everyone loved AnnaBelle; also, everyone was good to her. Pal loved her too, but her feelings for him never went beyond friendship, much to his dismay. He was such a nice guy, but her heart belonged to Joe, and only Joe. She would remain friends with Pal for a very long time.

Kathy and I didn't mind the move; we were always ready for a new adventure. I ended up having to quit my job at Borky's. It was probably in the nick of time, I think the salad lady, Mae, was buying my plane ticket to New Orleans. I hated to leave the security of my first job. I had been there for almost two years. I would miss having my own money, but I didn't seem to have the ambition to find another job closer to our new home. Kathy had never worked, and it was beginning to look unlikely that she ever would. We were seventeen and eighteen now, and we desperately needed to find a life with direction. Mom had been very patient, but even she had her limits. She didn't like lazy people, and believe me, we had lazy down to a science. My pastime was to sit and gaze out the windows. It was amazing what you could see. The apartment building was across the street from "The John Herron Art School". With the warm weather and mostly sunny days that year, the art students spent their time outside on the lawn with drawing and painting equipment. I liked watching them work, I don't know why, but I always thought about being in Paris. I just knew in my heart that some day I would travel overseas and see all the beautiful sights that waited there. I would visit all the castles in Europe, I love the mystery that surrounds these ancient homes. Then, of course, I would meet a prince, fall in love, and live *"happily ever after". (Why do I write poetry? Did you read the first book???)*

It was the summer of 1964, things were moving slowly for all three of us Bollan women, but life in general was fun. It was at this time that Kathy took a trip to Missouri to see our Uncle Bud and Aunt Darlene. Her trip would also reunite her with William and Effie Bollan, the Grandparents either of us barely knew. At the same time, I left with Grandpa Wicker for a short two week trip to Ohio. He needed to take care of some business. He and Grandma had moved back to Indiana by this time, they were living at Culver, Indiana. Their son, Raymond, had a Ford dealership there and wanted them closer to the family. They still owned the house in Ohio that needed attention from time to time; this was the reason for the trip. The two week trip turned into four weeks, but I didn't mind at all. I was with the one man in my life that meant the most to me, my Grandfather.

Kathy was home from Missouri when I returned from Ohio. She had been given information from Grandma Bollan about the three children from Dad's first marriage. Now we had addresses and phone numbers for the sister and brothers we didn't remember at all. We were both excited and a little scared, not knowing what sort of reaction we would receive when we contacted them. At long last we would come face to face with Don, Ted, and Janelle. First, Kathy wrote to Janelle. Hearing back from her immediately, we were happy they wanted to see us. Janelle made plans to come Indianapolis with her mother, Willodean, and stepfather, Dan Staggs. We would return to Wabash with them and stay for two weeks. Janelle lived at Wabash with her mom, Don and Ted both lived close by in Huntington.

AnnaBelle took this news rather well. She wasn't happy at the prospect, but she also knew she had to let us take this trip. The inevitable had finally come to pass. She always knew this day would come; the past would come back and bite her. What she couldn't have foreseen were the changes this trip would eventually bring. Our lives would never be the same. Be it good or bad, the times… they were a-changing.

Kathy and I stayed at Wabash with Janelle for the first few days. Don and Ted came down in the evenings and we all went to play miniature golf, we had so much fun with them. The second week was spent in Huntington at Ted's house. Janelle, Kathy and I all three slept in a full bed upstairs, like we were little kids, talking most of the night. We didn't sleep much, because we weren't little kids. We were big girls, there wasn't room to even turn over in that bed.

We finally had some answers about the mystery surrounding Dad. The five of us spent those two weeks getting to know each other, and catching up on life in general. Both Don and Ted were married with children. Don's wife was Lou, she is still the best sister-in-law ever. At that time they had four children, David, Mona, Angie, and Kent. They would later have Marcie, she would be their last. Ted was married to Susie, they had two kids, Sylvia and Dean. Janelle was planning her wedding to Jerry. Afterward, she too would live in Huntington.

There was one more life altering event that took place in Huntington during that first trip. Kathy and I were at Don's house on a Sunday afternoon. Two of his friends, Johnny and his cousin Mike, stopped by for a beer. As I sat there looking at the man called Johnny, I knew he was going to be the man I would marry. I had no idea how or when, I just knew it would happen. Sounds so simple doesn't it? As we all know, life can become very complicated. Did I mention he was, beyond any doubt, the best looking man I had ever seen?

The time went quickly, and before we knew it, we were back in Indy, with the heat of August bearing down on all of us. That little apartment was like living in the asphalt jungle, it was so hot. "I'm melting." Too bad I couldn't melt off the thirty pounds I had gained early that summer from eating banana splits at the corner drug store across the street. Not a pretty sight.

Shortly after our trip, Kathy moved to Chicago with friends. Mom didn't seem to mind too much, she couldn't have stopped her anyway. Her oldest daughter was eighteen and headstrong. A point of contention between the two of them for many years. Perhaps this was a blessing in disguise, maybe now they would be happy to see each other when she came home for visits. I certainly didn't mind, my life was changing too. I had never enjoyed the tension that could quickly develop between the two of them. Perhaps I was the only one that saw it, but I was also the one that had to live with it. I felt life would be better all the way around.

Not long after Kathy's move to Chicago, Mom and I moved again, renting the first floor of a house at 1814 N. Illinois Avenue. It was only three blocks from The Picadilly, but a far better place to live. The rooms were large and spacious, much larger than the tiny apartment we had been living in. For the first time in my life, I had a bedroom of my own. It was heaven. I always envied girls with their own rooms, not having to share their space. I put all my "stuff" everywhere. Then I bought more "stuff" just to make sure there was no room for anyone else's.

My happiness was increased because I loved this beautiful old home. There was something about the house that stay's in my memory, and it will continue to hold a special place in my heart. It was elegant, yet warm and inviting. Mom and I were happy there, it was a big house with plenty of room.

There were a few "incidents" while we lived there. Mainly the one that was highlighted in the first book. Much like "the night the lights went out in Georgia", it was "the night the drapes came down in Indy". I will repeat, AnnaBelle could be a scrappy little lady. Furthermore, AnnaBelle with a couple of cocktails in her could sometimes be more than anyone wanted to meet on a quiet night. I mean, for Gods sakes, all I wanted to do was sleep. (You have to read the first book to fully understand.) Trying again to avoid repetition … It concerned a dining room, red velvet drapes, chairs, newspapers, and the temper of AnnaBelle.

Shortly after we had moved and settled in, I decided to finally get a job, it was past due. I went to The G. C. Murphy Company, located one block off the circle in downtown Indy. They were hiring for the Christmas season, so I didn't have a problem. After a week of orientation, I started in the toy department. That was perfect, all the new toys were in, along with hundreds of huge *stuffed animals. Naturally I had to buy a few. They completely covered the spare twin bed in my room, I kept it that way in case anyone got any crazy ideas. There was no room at the inn. Selfish, yes. Sorry, no.*

    I walked the eighteen blocks to work in the morning, and took either a taxi or the bus home in the evening. It wasn't long until the thirty banana split pounds did melt off. I felt so much better. It was a good time, I loved Fall, and the coolness in the air. I briefly dated a co-worker named Jim. Not a good idea, that's why it was brief.

    I did take one quick trip to Huntington the end of September, continuing into the first week of October. I had pre-arranged it, so there wasn't a problem with my new job. I was to be Janelle's maid of honor at her and Jerry's wedding. The ceremony was beautiful, and so was the bride. I stayed with Ted and Susie for the rest of the week before returning to Indianapolis, they lived in a two story house on the outskirts of Huntington.

    I stayed busy with learning experiences the rest of the week. Don and Ted took me bowling, I didn't bowl. Ted took me squirrel hunting, I didn't hunt. We had a few beers, I didn't drink. They taught me to play Uker, I didn't know how. Come to think of it, I don't know how I lived without Uker. They treated me like the little sister I had always wanted to be. They were going to take me "snipe" hunting, had mercy and didn't. Like an idiot, I would have gone with them. The two of them went so far as to explain about how the "snipe" were these little creatures that you could only catch at night. You had to go in the woods with a paper bag, rattle it, and wait for them to run into it. I found out later they would leave the idiot holding the bag in the woods and make them walk home. Yes, give me a good snipe hunting trip any day of the week.

    They told me about Lu-Lar, the ghost that lived in the duct work at their Aunt Hazels house, they lived with her when they were small. Lu-Lar kept them in line when they were kids. Their worst fear was being put in the ducts. We all had our crosses to bear. They had Lu-Lar, we had Stovall. I think it was a toss-up.

(Thanks a- lot Dad.) I loved being there, and I missed them when I returned home.

It was the end of October, and the holidays were quickly approaching. Mom and I were having a great time in the new house. I painted the kitchen cabinets white, they needed it. (I still paint everything.) When the weather finally turned cold I took the bus to work and caught a cab home in the afternoon. I hated to give up walking, but it was getting daylight later, and the air was pretty cool that early in the morning. I worked during the day, Mom was still working late into the night. We spent our time together catching up on what had happened, usually when Mom came in from work she would wake me, and we talked. Except for the one night that I didn't want to talk, I was tired. In the end, I was sorry, very sorry. It was "The Night". I wouldn't talk to her, she got mad, very mad. She had drunk a few cocktails before leaving work, this was not uncommon. What happened next was. She tore down the dining room drapes, those red velvet drapes that I loved so much. Actually, it looked like a war zone when I got up the next morning to go to work. I walked back to her bedroom, just to wake her up and give her a dose of her own medicine. But there she lay, sleeping like an innocent baby. Really, she was as guilty as sin, but innocent as a newborn. Where's the justice? I left her sleeping. Don't think we didn't discuss that little episode. Not surprising, she didn't remember a thing. At least that's what she said.

Here again is the time for the cocktail party from hell. In case you didn't read this before, we'll just have a quick review of the facts. One morning around 4 or 5 AM Mom woke me from a sound sleep to tell me about the arrest that had taken place. She was beside herself with grief, crying and sobbing. The police had raided the club at Pals Lounge, arresting everyone that was present. Since it was a private club, the clientele consisted of politicians, lawyers, businessmen, and their wives. Yes, there was drinking after hours, yes, there was gambling in the back, yes, there was betting going on, but a raid? I still think Pal must have really gotten on someone's list, it had to be a judge. Only a scorned judge would have signed such a search warrant. And arresting everyone? Right down to the waitresses? I thought for sure that poor Mom was going to have the big one that night. "Fingerprinted, I was fingerprinted", she repeated it over, and over, and over again. You would have thought they shoved bamboo shoots under her fingernails. It took forever to calm her down. Of course, the drinks she had at work were still in her system, driving the drama queen in her forward. It was great. Not that she was arrested, but just the memory of how cute she was in all her felonious glory.

The charges were everything concerning a dive. Again, a dive??? What in the name of the almighty made Pals Club a dive is beyond me. I guess it must have been the gambling. The charges were owning, operating, frequenting, drinking, gambling, and oh yes, working, at a dive. They released everyone that same evening, no one served hard time except AnnaBelle, according to her that night. She finally calmed down and went to bed, she had to, they had already planned a cocktail party for the next afternoon and she had to get some sleep. Cocktails??

The infamous party started around 2PM on that Sunday, they had to have time go home and clean up. The cocktails flowed, so did the language. They were having their lawyers sue the city, they were going to protest, they were going to have the heads, and badges, of every officer involved in this travesty of injustice. What they were, was once again, full of alcohol. Yes, more alcohol. My personal favorite was the way they talked about having their lawyers do this and do that. I don't think they even realized that their attorneys were right there in the room with them. They were great people and it was great fun to watch them.

I personally received advice from an array of people that day. Pal was determined to make me understand why I should never marry a person with thin lips. He said they were exceptionally mean. Mean, mean people. Of course he had already had a few of those cocktails, but I knew he really believed this. I, on the other hand, believed that most of his ex-wives must have had thin lips, I definitely know they had a lot of his money.

They were all (I call them the "Famous Felons") scheduled to appear in court the following day, Monday. In the end, they didn't have to, all the charges were dropped. That's why I believe it was a retaliation raid. So, in the end, AnnaBelle didn't have to serve the hard time that she thought came with her fingerprinting escapade. All was right with the world again. They went back to owning, operating, gambling, betting, and working at that "dive" known as Pals Lounge.

The Christmas of 1964 was a happy one. Mom and I spent hours decorating the house. We went shopping at Murphy's and purchased all new Christmas decorations one evening in December. Mom had taken a rare night off work, so she could spend the evening with me. We enjoyed supper together at one of the restaurants downtown before our shopping spree. For the first time in ages we could take our time and relax. No one had to rush to work. This will always remain one of my most pleasant memories.

The G.C. Murphy Company had closed their doors to the public that evening, and opened the store for the employees and their families. We looked at everything, but only bought new Christmas decorations for the house. Our theme this year would be pale blue and white. We bought beautiful, sparkling ornaments and garland. There was a special scarf and new stockings for the large fireplace in the living room. We both loved this focal point, it was our first fireplace and it looked beautiful. Mom ordered a tree from the florist, and had it flocked white. It may sound selfish, but I have to say I loved having Mom to myself for a change. It was the happiest winter I think I had ever experienced. We always enjoyed the same things in life. Looking back, I can see how similar our lives were.

Kathy came home from Chicago two days before Christmas and spent the holiday with Mom and I. We had a wonderful visit, there would be no tension, no arguments, and none of the usual strained silence. There wasn't a lot of money for gifts, but we had never splurged on gifts anyway, so this was normal. The one thing Mom bought each of us was a new clock radio. We loved them. They could not only wake us up, but wake us to music. What will they think of next?

Kathy returned to Chicago after the holidays, Mom and I returned to work and the routine we had gotten used to. Things were good, times were good. Not one of us could foresee how drastic our lives would change by the next Christmas. We all live for the "moment" when we are young, as we should. Worries will come with age and change, whether we like it or not. Looking back now, I see what a wonderful and exciting life I had with Mom. Even now I can close my eyes and my mind drifts back to that house. I'm with her again, just the two of us. But for the moment, I have to move forward.

The following March, I decided to take off work for one week and visit Don, Ted and Janelle. I took a bus to Huntington and Don met me at the station. I stayed with Ted and Susie again during this trip. Since my last visit they had moved to town and now lived just around the corner from Don and Lou. Janelle and her new husband, Jerry, lived with his mother, Rose, across town. Now that they all lived in the same town, visiting was easier.

Don had a party at his house that Friday night. He invited the man called Johnny, the man I had met eight months earlier. It seems he was one of Don's best friends. I learned that night he had just celebrated his 24th birthday. Even though I was just seventeen, I absolutely fell in love with him. We didn't really even carry on a conversation that night, but before the night was over, he sat down on the couch beside me, and kissed me. Of course, he doesn't remember it, he had consumed more than a few bottles of beer. I, on the other hand, did not. (Melting, I'm melting.) I still didn't know how, or when, but I knew this man was going to be my husband.

I returned to Indianapolis with the secret of Johnny in my mind. I never mentioned him to anyone, not even Mom, especially Mom. Probably because Johnny was not only six years older than me, but also divorced with three children. This alone would strike fear in the heart of any girl's mother. However, AnnaBelle wasn't just any girl's mother, I was her baby, and she could be fiercely protective. So, for once in my life, I chose to keep my thoughts to myself.

Time passed quickly the next two months. Then, my AnnaBelle's worst nightmare took place. My brother Ted called to ask if I wanted to move to Huntington and stay with him and Susie. Ted promised he would take good care of me, and pay me each week for babysitting with their two small children while they worked. Of course, I wanted to go, but Mom wasn't so sure it was the right decision. What I couldn't see, and Mom couldn't help but see, was that this was more than a visit. Even though Ted had promised to watch over every thing I did, Mom still carried a dread with her. She not only feared what may happen to me, but also dreaded the thought of being alone. We were close, closer that most mothers and daughters would ever be, we were best friends.

In the end, I left to go to Huntington. Mom stayed at the big house alone, keeping everything as it had been in my room, I'm sure she was hoping for a quick return. She didn't know about the man called Johnny. Had she known, things would have ended differently, I know in my heart I would not have been allowed to leave. I was, after all, still only seventeen.

Mom was dating Joe, they were together most of the time. He began to spend more time with her at home, now that she was alone. He was still working on that messy divorce, things were never easy. They did, however have a deep love for each other, and this was the driving force behind their relationship. Unfortunately, they both loved the nightlife, and all it had to offer, including the cocktail parties. Without either of us girls living at home to keep her grounded, Mom's life began to take on a different aspect. This was all good for a couple of years, but eventually, it would catch up with both her and Joe. I'm getting ahead of myself.

They were a beautiful couple, he was tall and handsome, she was small, and so attractive. He was suave, she looked like a movie star, it was a match made in heaven. Everything that is, except for the jealousy. That could be a living hell, especially when you mix it with alcohol. Kathy and I didn't know about the violence that could erupt between Mom and Joe, at least, not for a while.

There was one funny episode that Mom told me about. In his jealousy, Joe would suspect her of seeing someone else at the house on the nights they weren't together. On one such night, he parked his car about a block from the house, so he could go undetected and see what she was doing. He got a stepladder from the garage out back and set it by the dining room window so he could stand on it to see what was going on inside. All he saw was AnnaBelle turn off the lights and go to bed. Unfortunately, he lost his balance, fell off the ladder, almost broke his leg, and then had to lay there for about an hour before he could get up. He would give himself away if he yelled for help. Eventually he told on himself and they both had a good laugh.

I came home for short, week-end visits, but never long enough to satisfy Mom. She wanted me to come back home to stay, but that wasn't going to happen. I celebrated my eighteenth birthday in Huntington, little did Mom know with whom I would spend it.

At first, I started seeing Johnny occasionally. He didn't stop by the house very often, he was usually at the bar after work in the evening. (At the time he was working for the State Highway Department, as a surveyor.) On my birthday, however, things would change, I started seeing him much more often. All this was much to Ted's, dismay. Johnny may have been Don's best friend, but at that time, he wasn't Teds. Although Ted liked him, he didn't like him with his sister. He was older, divorced, and not the most grounded person. Ted felt responsible, even though there was little he could do. Ted and I were very close, I loved him very much, we spent so much time together I felt as though he had been with me all my life. Eventually that would change somewhat. Not the love, that will remain forever. He was there when I needed him, just as any big brother would be.

For the two weeks prior to my birthday, Johnny would tell Don that he was going to stop by Teds to see me, then not show up. It was disturbing, but not the end of the world. The night of my birthday, again, he wasn't there. A friend of Johnny's stopped by, took pity on me, and asked if I wanted to go for a ride and get a cup of coffee. Since my dance card wasn't exactly full, I gladly went. Huntington is a small town, made even smaller when we passed the familiar Lincoln while driving up Jefferson Street, the main "drag". Johnny owned a one-of-a-kind 1957 Lincoln, it was two-toned peach and cream colored. Hard to miss him on the street. (Remember that quiet thing with him? Well his car wasn't.) I didn't see his face, but the friend did. Grandpa used to talked about "Forty days of stormy weather", I think that described the look. He was furious. Although, at that time, I was unaware of Johnny's true nature, the friend wasn't. I'm pretty sure he saw his life flash before his eyes when the two cars passed on the street.

In the blink of an eye, I was driven to Don's house, which was fine with me. It seemed the evening had suddenly taken a dark turn. Don was in the middle of trying to explain Johnny to me when the man himself, and his Lincoln pulled up in front of the house. Drinking and driving obviously wasn't an issue with this man. He asked me if I wanted to go for a ride and have coffee. God, is that all these people knew .... coffee? A milk shake would have been nice. Like an idiot, a young one, but still an idiot, I left with him. After that night, the rest is history. He was at Ted's house every evening to see me. We spent that spring and summer lost in the dream world that only young love ever shares. It was wonderful. In the end, he became good friends with Ted.

By the middle of June, I thought I may be "expecting". I was also expecting Mom to be pretty ticked off. I was right on both counts. It wasn't exactly what I had planned for my life, I had lost my plans when I met Johnny, now he seemed to be the plan. I knew Mom wouldn't take this news well, unfortunately, I was right. Not only was her baby having a baby, she was with a man claiming to be divorced, with three children. This had to be some terrible trick, all she could think of was David Otto Bollan, aka Don Bollan, aka divorced. She demanded to see the divorce papers, just to prove it was true. I assured her that everything was okay. I had met the ex-wife, she was remarried with yet more children. There was nothing left to do but go forward with plans for a wedding.

My brother Don wrote a beautiful song for my wedding. He named it "Our Wedding Day" at the time. I love the music, and the *words have a special meaning for me. Unfortunately, he couldn't come to our wedding, so I never had the honor of having it done there. But just knowing it was special for me is enough. He has performed it numerous times at different wedding ceremonies, people love the song. I do have it recorded, I still love hearing him sing it.*

The date was set for August 1, 1965. It was a small wedding. I wanted the ceremony to be held at the house that I loved so much, Mom conceded, but demanded we be married by a minister, not a justice of the peace. This was fine, Johnny and I both just wanted it over and done with. There were few people in attendance, but it was still a beautiful ceremony. Grandma and Grandpa were both there, that was the most important thing. Kathy was my maid of honor and Grandpa gave me away, it was perfect.

I remember feeling, at the last minute, this overpowering sense of remorse, I just couldn't go through with this. Grandpa and I were standing in the bedroom that I loved so much. Me in my wedding dress, him in his suit, everyone else waiting in the other room. I was standing there with my arm through his, when I told him I couldn't do it. He turned to me and said, "Carolyn Sue, if you can't, you can't. Get your duds changed as fast as you can, get out the back door, and I'll hold them off as long as I can." What a Grandpa. End the end, both of us took a deep breath, opened the doors, and walked through them together.

Mom and Joe left for vacation the day after the wedding. They were headed for Florida. She had never lost her love for the "Sunshine State". They had a wonderful trip. Mom deserved a vacation. She had let me go to make my own life in the world, I know how hard that was for her. We stayed at the house in Indianapolis for a few days before heading back to Huntington. However, I still didn't pack all my things and take them with me. I took most of my clothes, but nothing else. There was a part of me that couldn't cut the ties with Mom, leaving my things would insure I still had a home with her.

Jack and AnnaBelle   1962

AnnaBelle at the Time Trials   1963

AnnaBelle at the State Fair   1963

AnnaBelle and Joe   1964

Carolyn Sue and John   1965

Chapter VIII

We All Move On..... With No Direction

It was only one short month after my wedding that Mom told me her and Joe were moving to Hollywood, Florida. They would do all of the packing, including the rest my belongings. Since he worked long hours during the week, Johnny and I would go down to Indy that following week-end to pick up my things. Mom was a clean freak, a trait she inherited from Grandma. Since my room had set empty with no cleaning for a while, she cleaned everything as they packed it. I really did appreciate this, except for my 45's (records). She washed them, "because they were dusty". I found them mostly a little warped, but clean, very, very, clean. It's amazing what warm soapy water, verses a dry soft cloth, can do to vinyl.

The house I loved so much was going the way of the wreaking ball within a month. The hospital had purchased the ground for yet another parking lot. Since the owner had no direct heirs, except a niece on the east coast, most of the contents were left. There was a huge safe in the basement, we spent an entire day trying to open the darn thing. I just knew it held treasures beyond belief. I'm sure it's still buried under the rubble, somewhere under the parking lot. (That would be in the 1800 block of N. Illinois Avenue, Indianapolis, In., if anyone's interested. Stupid hospital.) There were so many treasures in that house. In hind site, I wish I had taken some of them. At least I would have appreciated them.

When I left the house for the last time, I took all of my belongings with me. Looking back, it saddens me even now. As much as I loved my husband and my new life with him, I also loved what I was leaving behind. It just didn't feel right. I would find years later that there was a reason for my uneasiness, cutting all ties leaves nothing to go home to.

As I sorted through my possessions, and put things away, I came across the letters that would alter my marriage forever. They were just letters, love letters yes, but just words on a page. I guess I should have destroyed them two years earlier, but it never occurred to me that anyone else would have reason to read them. I didn't even realize they were packed in the boxes, they had simply slipped my mind. When Mom packed my things, too bad she didn't wash these along with those records. This story is also in the first book, so I won't dwell on it. Long story short, Johnny read them all, lost his mind, hated me for a few weeks, made my life miserable, and was generally a real ass about the whole thing.....then he burned them. I guess he thought I had never dated another man, never kissed another man, or ever felt any emotion what-so-ever before he came along. Yes, I came straight from the nunnery, that must have been what he wanted to believe. Sure, just like I wanted to believe he had stepped out of the priesthood the day I met him. THEY WERE JUST LETTERS. I know, let it go.....

On the up side, Mom gave us the Curtis Mathis television/ stereo console. I was thrilled. Since we had little money, we didn't have a television, radio, or stereo. It didn't really matter to me, but it was so nice to be able to listen to the radio. Not to mention, I could play my records again. Well, the ones that weren't wavy. She didn't wash my albums, they were all still in their covers. My Johnny Mathis was safe. They called them dust covers for a reason. The reason was Mom.

Mom and Joe lived in Florida about seven months before moving back to Indy. I know they had a wonderful time while living there. Mom worked at a cocktail lounge there, she told me about meeting Jackie Gleason. He would be another person that asked for Mom when he came into the lounge. He reminded her of her brother, Ray. He did tease her all the time, but he also left her outrageous tips. She commented that he spent money like he was "pouring water out of a bucket". I believe he played golf in the area. She said he was funny, and kind to her. But he could also be insulting to some of the people he was with.

Joe brought Mom home for Thanksgiving that year. Johnny and I went to Culver, Indiana, as did Mom, to spend the day with Grandma and Grandpa. Including the two of them, there were only eight of us there. My three cousins, Kim, Jeff, and Corky were there because their mother had left them in the care of our Grandparents for the weekend. We had a wonderful day with everyone. Joe had brought Mom to Culver that morning. He returned to pick her up around 4 PM.

My Grandparents home was on the lake, with a pier going out into the water. Johnny had taken his fishing pole, one of his passions was fishing. While they were out on the pier that afternoon Grandpa told my husband why he didn't fish. He said he tried it once, and only once. He decided to go when he was about nine year's old, back in Kentucky. He found a long, fairly straight, thin piece of a tree limb, put a line and hook on it, and took off for the river. His first cast out resulted in a tug on the line. He said he jerked as hard as he could on the pole. This huge eel flew out of the water, and wrapped around his neck. He dropped the pole, started screaming, and while desperately grabbing at the eel, ran all the way home. If Grandpa said it happened, it happened

That year I didn't spend Christmas with Mom, it was my first without her. It wouldn't be the last, but one of only a few. She always tried to make it home for our favorite holiday. I missed her, but life went on. I was pretty busy making a mess of my own life.

We lost Edgil on March 1, 1966, due to a massive heart attack. He was 59 years old. It was six months to the day after he walked me through those double doors and into the arms of my husband. It was one week after I gave birth to his first great-grandchild, the child he would never see, or tease, or tell his stories to. I know it is selfish to speak only of my feelings, his loss broke the hearts of many. We each celebrate his life in different ways, for different reasons. But the emptiness he left in my life was almost more than I could bear. His memory still brings tears to my eyes. I still smell his Old Spice, I still feel his presence, this is my only comfort.

Losing Grandpa is also what brought Mom back to Indiana. She wanted to be close to Grandma, this was the one person for which there was no comfort. Grandpa was her life, and her only life. For the family, the grief over his death would be compounded less than three months later with the passing of Grandma on May

15, 1966, at the age of 58. There are no words to describe the pain of all those left behind. Again, I sit here alone, but the tears begin to flow. They say she died because of pneumonia, a complication of the leukemia she was diagnosed with after the loss of her Edgil. But we all know it was due to her broken heart, the heart that could never recover after Grandpa was gone. As sad as the tears may sound, they are also a tribute to how loved these two people were. And, a tribute to their memory for all of us.

The next few months are fully covered in book one, so I'm not going to elaborate on them. It would be too repetitive for those that read it. For those who haven't, you'll have to fill in the blanks. Like the blanks where I turn into the pregnant young bride from hell, jealous and hormonal. I receive a letter from the mother of Johnny's supposed "love child", which I knew nothing about, heard way too many stories from his first wife, the mother of his first three daughters, and generally felt that life really wasn't "Some Enchanted Evening" after all. I know you're asking yourself how all this could be happening, what with him being a man of the cloth and all. And let's not forget quiet, yes, very, very quiet. Too bad everyone else wasn't as quiet as he was.

It all comes down to that one saying, "What a tangle web we weave, when first we practice to deceive". You knew I could never just leave it there, don't act so surprised. It's hard to understand why there wasn't one person that could tell me some truth about the man I was getting ready to marry while we were still dating. Well, I take that back, Ted tried. I really believed he was talking about the drinking and the fighting. I knew that wouldn't be an ongoing problem, and it wasn't. But, if I really stop and think about some of the little things that took place while we were dating, I would have seen a part of the man that I didn't want to see. Looking back now, I know that I stupidly blocked things from my mind. "There are none so blind, as he who will not see". You think????

I had been dating Johnny about a month when my sister, Janelle, told me she and her husband were out driving around and passed us out by the bowling ally. She wondered why I didn't wave to her, she said they honked and everything, even told me the time. I simply said I didn't see them. Now, in the sinking bottom of my heart, I knew I wasn't with him by the bowling ally, on that evening, at that particular time. I was with him later, just as I was every evening. So, I buried it in my mind. But, I forgot to bury the shovel I buried it with. (Remember, I told you, you must always bury the shovel you buried it with?) Janelle did let me know later that she was trying to tell me Johnny had been with another woman, she knew it wasn't me in the car. Well, drop a brick on my head the next time. He was actually with the mother of the child that was said to belong to him. Unfortunately, we were already married by the time I found out. Was he grilled? As the judge says. "like a cheeseburger". He actually lived through every man's worst nightmare, being accused by a teenaged, pregnant, jealous, bitchy wife. Oh, yes, I was all that and more. He finally said he was telling her that he couldn't see her again, he loved me and we were getting married. Okay ....whatever.

Then, the other shovel I forgot to bury came back and bit him on the ass, in more ways than one. He had played softball for the Show Lounge in Huntington for years. I went to all his games with him that spring and summer. Sometimes I would sit in the bleachers, most times I sat in his car. He always parked so I could see the field clearly. On one such night, he came over to the car after the game and threw his mitt in the back seat, never said a word to me, then he left with one of the other players. Ted and Janelle were usually at the games with their families. Ted played for Utrad, the factory where he worked. They all saw Johnny leave, Ted wanted me to go home with them, I wouldn't go. I told him Johnny would be right back. He probably went for a beer. I sat in the car for about two hours when Janelle and Jerry came back to get me. This time I left with them and went home. His excuse later was that he did go for that beer, and I was gone when he got back. Unfortunately, the friend he left with couldn't keep his mouth shut forever, yet still, he waited until after we were married to open it. It seemed he took my future husband to a party to introduce him to a girl that had been wanting to meet him. But, the friend said, Johnny loved me so much that he drank too much and fell asleep in a chair.

What's wrong with these people??? This time I really did have "stupid" tattooed across my forehead. In big red letters. And yet, people wondered why I didn't trust him. Why was I so jealous? But worse yet, I got the impression that my husband also thought I had no reason to be upset. Oh, the humanity..... just shoot me now.

Shortly after Johnny and I were married, Kathy came for a visit. She had decided Chicago wasn't the place for her after all. She asked if she could stay with us until she could find a job and get her own place. It wasn't the best decision for our young and troubled marriage; it could be very uncomfortable most of the time. She had no way of knowing about all the turmoil that was affecting both of us at the time. However, it didn't take her long to find a job, get her own apartment, and start making friends. Our brother, Ted, helped her with the job. She was hired at what was then, "Utrad", in 1966.

She ended up being a big help after the birth of our daughter, Jenny. For the first few days, she would stay with me at night while Johnny was away at work.

Mom and Joe had moved back to Indianapolis by the first of the year, 1966. They lived in Florida a short time, only about four months. It worked out well for me; Mom was able to get to the hospital when I had the baby. She was a little late, but made it. At that time, I thought Mom and Joe were both so happy, but I didn't see them often. Unfortunately, things weren't going so well. Maybe I would have understood if I hadn't been so wrapped up in my own version of a "relationship".

Kathy became restless by that following summer. For some unknown reason, she decided to join the military. I believe it was in June that she enlisted in the Army. June of 1966 was not the time most individuals wanted to be in the service. The Vietnam War was raging, as were the tempers of those involved with the anti-war movement. As the war continued, we came to know the depth of the affect on the youth of this country. Draft dodging became a familiar and very controversial term.

More controversy evolved by the early 1970's. Woodstock was the rage. As were demonstrations, flower children, communes, sit-ins, pot, and free sex. We were introduced to mini- skirts, maxi-skirts, bell bottoms, paisley prints, and Sonny and Cher. Then, along with the pot, came bongs, roach clips, LSD, angel dust, and any number of mind altering drugs. Of course there was the peace sign. I'm pretty sure that was introduced by someone that was so "strung out" they couldn't argue anymore. "Peace Man" said it all.

I'm forced to mention the burning of the bra's here. Come on, was that really necessary? We all saw some really scary things at the time, but some women without their bra should never have been on the list. Again, what were they thinking? If it feels good do it? That may be true, but as true as it is, do it alone in your own home for the sake of God. Have some mercy on the rest of us. You're an embarrassment, grow up, get over it, and let it go. Seriously, it just wasn't right. When it looked bad, it was really, really bad. Moving on.

Kathy went to Indianapolis to spend her last civilian night with Mom before going off to boot camp. She rose early the next morning, as did Mom. They were just pouring their coffee when Joe broke down the front door to the apartment. He was drunk, very drunk. It was obvious he had been at it all night. He rushed over to Mom, threw her to the floor, and began kicking her. Before a shocked Kathy could react, the situation quickly worsened. He was screaming and then cursing at the woman we both thought he loved so much. Then, in a heartbeat, Kathy drew back her fist and hit him between the eyes. Actually, she floored him, literally. She broke his glasses, but it was enough to stop the assault on her Mother. I believe it was also pretty sobering. That's not really a cheap shot, we all know he felt it. He told Kathy that we two girls didn't know the things Mom could do to drive him crazy. She told him in no uncertain terms that it didn't matter what she did, she was our Mother. It wasn't the happy send-off her daughter should have had, but AnnaBelle thanked God Kathy was there at that moment in time.

Mom and Joe worked things out. They remained in Indy for another month and then moved to Ardmore Pennsylvania, a suburb on the west side of Philadelphia. They had decided to start over in a new location, away from everyone. They found a nice apartment, settled in and then started looking for jobs. Joe went to work in insurance, a field he had always done well in. Mom found employment at a high end retail store in the make-up department. This would suit her style, she had the face to perfectly demonstrate the make-up. From the letters I received, all seemed right with the world again. I was happy for them, I had always known how deep their love was, but now I also knew about the jealousy that plagued the relationship. Most of it was due in part to the cocktail parties and the clubs they would frequent. But that went along with the lifestyle and the people they encountered in the businesses they were in.

Mom and Joe stayed in Pennsylvania for about three years. Those were the same three years Kathy was in the service. I'm not sure how smooth things were between them, Mom never said too much when she came home, but I could see she wasn't as happy as she used to be. I know what finally caused the beginning of the end for them. Mom had someone come to visit her. (I will not say who it was, she knows who she is.) This was a person that she loved, not only loved, but trusted. You know the saying about keeping your friends close, and your enemies closer? This is a perfect example of what this can mean.

Mom had to work late the night her visitor flew in at the airport, so Joe agreed to go alone to pick her up. Mom would be home by the time they arrived back at the apartment. She wondered at the time why they were late getting back. Joe said something about the traffic, and it was forgotten. They had a wonderful visit. There were lunches, cocktail parties, and sightseeing trips around Philadelphia. One thing AnnaBelle loved to do was entertain, she was in her element. All in all, it was a wonderful week.

Unfortunately when it was time for the return trip to the airport, again, Mom had to work. So Joe was nice enough to volunteer to transport their guest back to her return flight. Mom had been home *from work for quite some time before Joe returned. She knew in her heart that something had happened to keep him. They had a couple of drinks and she began to question him. I can't begin to imagine what went though her mind when he finally confessed. Yes, he had cheated. (Once again, proving why some men are filthy animals.) Both of these people that she loved so much had betrayed her. Not just once, but twice. They had not been held up in traffic when he picked her up, they were held up in a motel room. The same thing happened on the return trip to the airport, apparently at the same motel. I wonder if it was the "No tell Motel"? Sorry, bad joke, even though Mom would laugh at that too.*

Years later, when Mom told me this story, I was livid. She could never forgive Joe, and probably never completely forgave the other woman. She continued to associate with her until the end, but I never knew why. I guess she felt she had to. I remain steadfast in my belief that neither of them should have ever been able to look at themselves in the mirror again. I have never forgiven this woman for breaking the heart of my Mother, and I doubt I ever will. But as for this "other woman", it wasn't the first time she had done this, and I doubt there will ever be a last. Not as long as she has no conscience, no heart, and the morals of an ally cat. Bitter..... yes, I'm bitter.

This incident happened about the same time Kathy was discharged from the Army. This was also discussed in the first book, along with my opinion of the Vietnam War. Anyway, Kathy drove to Pennsylvania, picked up Mom and her belongings, and they drove west. Their final destination was San Francisco. Could they have gone any farther? Well, I would have loved to visit Hawaii, but that wasn't on their agenda.

I think it was about three days after they had left Pennsylvania that Joe called me. Evidently, Mom had left without telling him she was going. I didn't blame her, but I could hear the pain in his voice. He kept telling me how much he loved her, and begged me to tell him where she was. I assured him that she wasn't with me, but she was safe. He finally understood that I couldn't tell him anything, it wasn't my place to do so. I really hated that they split up; they had loved each other for such a long time, and went through so much to be together. This is why I will never forgive the person that brought this about, never. I blame Joe too, but some women are just evil, this one is especially so.

The trip went well, there was only one incident. They stopped for gas and food before they started across the desert. When they left there, for some unknown reason, Mom's purse was on the roof of the car. She didn't miss it for hours. Needless to say, Kathy wasn't going back for it. I would rather drive back through a hail storm, than suffer with Moms emotion over losing her purse and everything inside. She was always worried about losing it, now it had happened. There was no calming her, she was beside herself. I'm not sure she ever forgave Kathy for not turning around, and I certainly wasn't going to ask. Some things are better left alone. Again, bury it. From then on, we all kept a close watch on any purse Mom happened to be carrying. If she would misplace it for even a moment, she would start to panic. She always carried half her life inside them. Not only was her wallet in it, there would be pictures, tissues, medication, makeup, gum, combs, rubber bands, keys, a bottle of water, and last, but not least, a small package of crackers in case someone got hungry. We could have lived for days on the contents of Mom's purse. And yet, she wondered why her shoulders hurt.

Arriving in San Francisco represented a new, fresh start for both of them, and, a bit of a challenge. They both had to find work and a place to live. A job for Mom was easy to find, she started work at DiMaggio's Restaurant, located on Fisherman's Wharf. It seems she and Kathy stopped in there for coffee shortly after they arrived in the city. Mom was looking her best, as usual. Joey DiMaggio (Joe's nephew), was standing at the bar, she went over to him and started asking him about work. She was hired that day, and started as a cocktail waitress the next. In the end, waitressing seemed to be her forte. Eventually, Kathy would also come to work at DiMaggio's. She was a cashier, a job that suited her well. Not surprisingly, they quickly became favorites of the DiMaggio family.

Mother and daughter both were hard working, attractive women, and an asset for the business.

Joey DiMaggio would become a close friend of Mom's, but because he was married, it would never go any farther. They would share many adventures together, and he would regularly fire her. Of course, the next morning he had to call her, only to hire her back. This became a ritual, a regular part of the job.

One night after work, Joey decided he could do what no man had done before, teach AnnaBelle to operate a moving vehicle. Foolish man. I know bigger and better men had tried before, and failed miserably. I'm not counting Larry, he was neither bigger, nor better. I have to wonder how many cocktails it took for Joey to let her get behind the wheel of his new Caddy. In the end, the front bumper of his car became best friends with a light pole located on the wharf. Again, she was fired, again, he called the next morning. It's too bad they could never be more than friends. They would have made such a cute couple. Unlike his Uncle Joe, Joey was rather short, but very good looking.

Joey would be the man chosen to give the bride away when Kathy was married in 1970. I made the trip to San Francisco, along with my children, for the blessed event. This, too, is in the first book. Most of it anyway. John and I were at a really bad place in our marriage, the trip did nothing to help that. It did however, help me to face some harsh realities about my life, and my husband. Realities such as, you're an ass, I hate you for living, if you were drowning I would pray for rain, if you were on fire I would pray for lightening, and finally, you suck. In summing it up, I would say this, "you're annoyed, I'm annoyed, together we're a paranoid". He didn't want me to go to San Francisco, and he could not hurt me any more than he did while I was there. When he told me not to bother coming home, it was the one time in his life, he really needed to be quiet.

There were some funny and enjoyable moments during my visit to San Francisco. Mom and I spent one day with her friends, Claude and Gladys, sightseeing. They were such a nice couple, and so patient with the kids. We visited Seal Island, Chinatown, took in the Zoo, and had lunch at a nice café. We stopped in at the bar where Charles (The groom) worked, to visit. This is where Jenny made her singing debut with "Julie, Julie, Julie, Do You Love Me" by Bobby Sherman. She was singing along with the song while standing on a barstool. Okay, she was only four years old, but the bar was closed. I took my children to only the best places to stand on barstools and sing. Johnny, at nine months, would take his first steps while we were in San Francisco, which thrilled both Mom and I.

The day of the wedding is etched in my memory. I was Kathy's maid of honor, while our cousin Liz was a bridesmaid. Liz and I changed into our dresses at the church before the ceremony. We had both been to final fittings the week before, but when we stepped out of the dressing room, neither of us looked quite right. I didn't really care at the moment, I had a raging hangover from the party the night before. What were we thinking, the night before???? Mom could have killed me. Anyway, we stood there for a couple of minutes when Joey finally said, "You girls know you have each others dresses on, right?" Liz was really big busted, me, not so much. Therefore, the top of my dress just hung on me, while Liz looked like she had a binder on. He said to hurry and switch dresses. Switch I could do, hurry wasn't going to happen. I did well to change the first time, God, my head was spinning. Plus, the dresses were olive green, not a good color at any time. Evidently, in 1970, olive green was "the color". The ceremony started a few minutes late, but all was well.

Mom looked beautiful, as always. She loved planning for the wedding, and having me there with the kids, it was the first time she had met her grandson, she hadn't been home for sometime now. The reception was on a grand scale. It was a gift to Kathy from the DiMaggio family, and it was quite an event. The champagne flowed, way too fast in my opinion, but never-the-less, it flowed. The party went on for hours. Actually, I think it lasted longer than Kathy's marriage to Charles. But that's not my story to tell. I had problems of my own.

We recently found a letter packed in all of Mom's mementos, it was from Joe. It had been mailed to her in San Francisco. We had no idea there was ever any contact between them after she left Pennsylvania, but there was. I was happy and relieved to see it. I knew they had always loved each other, and that cemented my hopes. She never seriously dated anyone after their break-up, I guess she was never ready to make that kind of commitment again. The letter starts with, "Dear Izzy", one of his pet names for her. He said she wasn't blonde, but she was dizzy. Maybe I will enter it in the book; I don't think she would have minded.

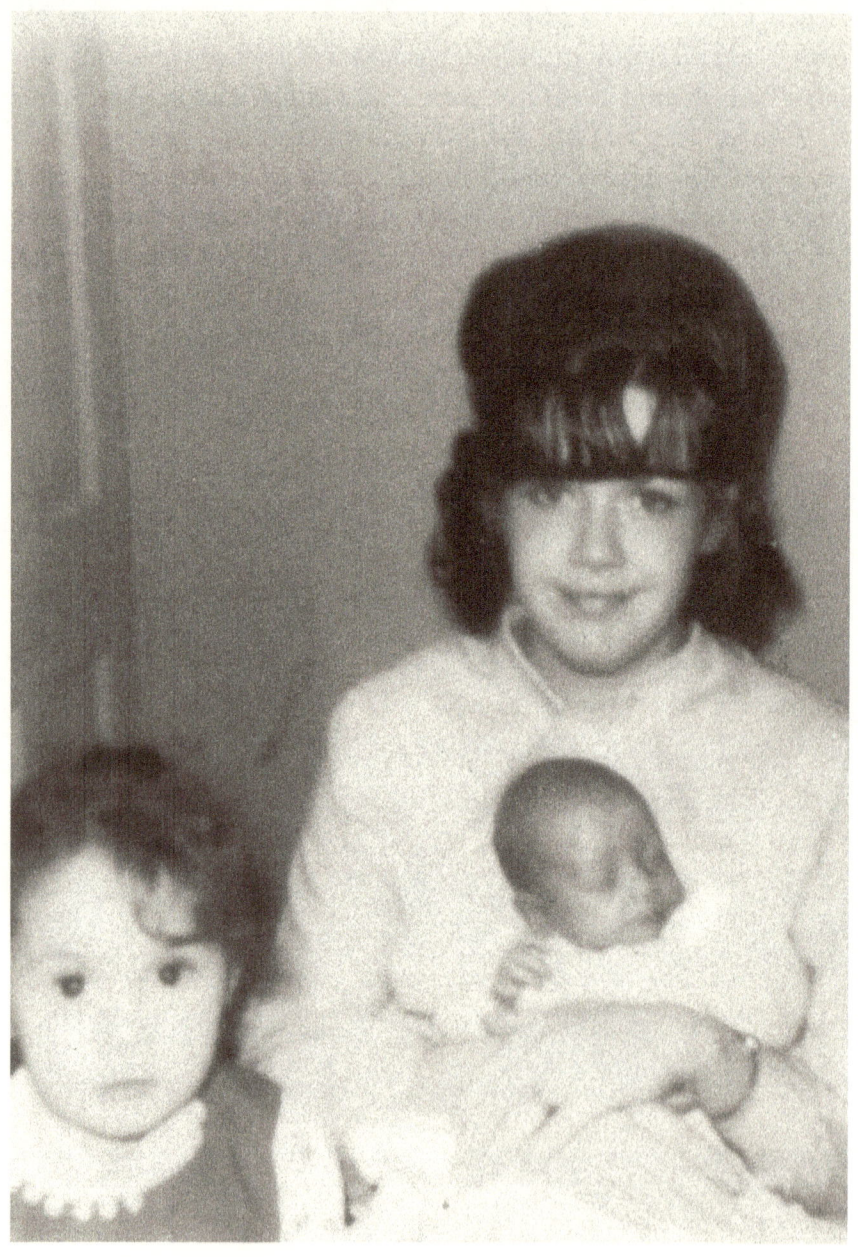

1969
Carolyn Sue with Jenny, age 3, and Johnny, age 1 month.

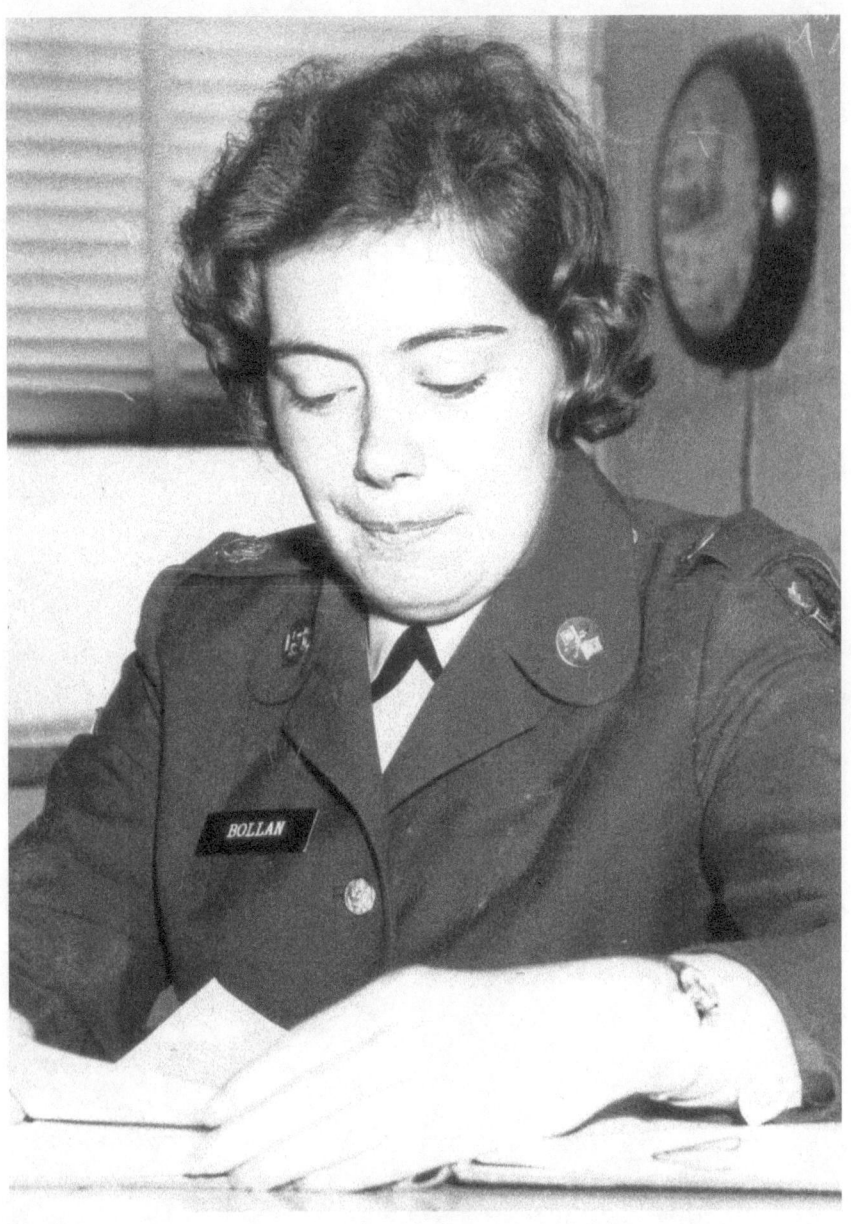

Kathy   1968
Fort Rucker , Alabama

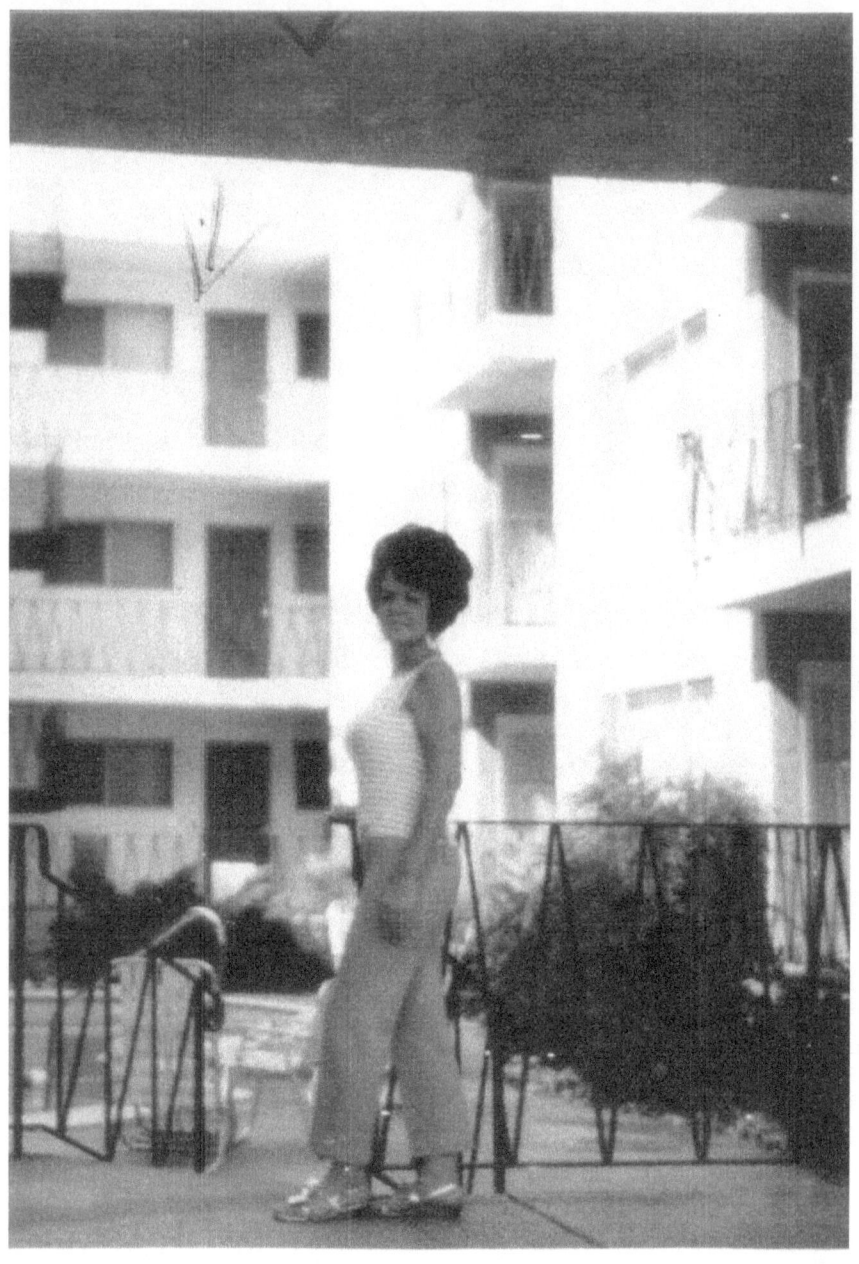

AnnaBelle   1969
San Francisco

Chapter IX

Back Home Again, In Indiana

After I returned home from San Francisco I went through some mind and marriage alterations. (As told in book one.) We had been married for almost 5 years. It had to happen sooner or later I suppose. It wasn't that I was unhappy with the man; it was the circumstances that were killing everything I had felt. My love for John was as strong as the dream world I was living in. Both had a reality check, both paid in the end.

I vividly remember the good times as well as the bad. And I try very hard not to dwell on the latter. Therein lays the secret, facing that what's done is done. If you accept things and move on, keep moving. It's difficult not to re-visit the issues and think "if I had it to do over, I would do this, or say that". There are no do-over's in real life, only in our dreams, so keep them there. "Know when to hold them, know when to fold them". I needed a new deck of cards. I had been playing solitaire for a very long time.

John was not a person to be taken lightly, he worked hard, at everything he did. Our fights and arguments were far and few between. Mainly because I still didn't like confrontation. Unfortunately, I had enough of AnnaBelle in me that when we fought, we fought. Well, I did. The outcome was always the same, we made up. The majority of our battles came about when we were drinking, which we seldom did back then, thank God. One of us wouldn't have made it if we had been drinking regularly. Looking back, some of the "spats" are funny now. Our problems almost always evolved at a party. Why? Because there was always alcohol at a party. We finally quit going to them, I think everyone there outgrew them. .

One such occasion happened at Jack and Linda's house. They are mentioned in the first book, they were a major part of our lives, and our best friends. They remain, and always will be, close in my heart. The growing years of our youth, and our marriage were spent with them, I even wore Linda's wedding veil as my borrowed during my own wedding ceremony. I didn't know her at the time, my sister Janelle did, and borrowed it for me. In the end it was fate. Jack and Linda were married in June and our wedding was in August of 1965, our lives would be intertwined for years. Linda became the third best friend I had in my life, and the third Linda. Moving on. (God, how I ramble, you'd think it was age, but alas, I've done it all my life.) Again, moving on.

We were all sitting around the kitchen table talking. (At the party) Yes, it was the talk of alcohol. The conversation led to women they had all known, and eventually led to a girl that was "loose". John made the comment that he respected her because she wouldn't "go out" with him, and that she was the only one he did respect. He knew this girl before I even met him, and I still didn't know her. That may have been part of my problem, Huntington was a fairly small town, everybody we knew had grown up together. I sometimes felt like an outsider, well, I was. And I was definitely out of the loop. But not that night, I made my own loop. Naturally, I took his comment personally. Had he been sober, he would have thought before speaking, or at least chose his words more carefully. Had I been sober, I would still have reacted they way I did. In an instant I reached across the table and slapped his face. Now, what was I thinking? Oh, I don't know. Maybe it was about the ride with the old girlfriend, or perhaps it the party where he went to meet another girl. Anyway, while I watched my life flash before my eyes, you could have heard a pin drop in that room. Everyone, including me, knew his temper well. He reached across the table, grabbed the front of my blouse, and pulled me across the top of the table. Nose to nose, through gritted teeth, he quietly said "don't ever do that again". Even though I was still more than a little mad at him, I knew how lucky I had been. We never found the buttons that he ripped off my blouse.

Then, there was the time a few months later, when we were all at our house for Linda's birthday party. It was the end of a very hot August in 1969. I was pregnant, a little over six months pregnant with our son, Johnny. Naturally, I wasn't drinking. Needless to say, everyone else was. I was sitting at the kitchen table by the open window, talking to John's sister, Pat. He came into the room with some smart remark, I don't remember what it was, the mood I was in it may have been "hello". All I could think about was him being gone each weekend, every weekend, golfing or fishing. This went on through the entire spring and summer every year. The thing about him working ten hour days, five days a week seemed to slip my mind. In a moment of insanity, without thinking, I threw a glass of water in his face. Stupid, stupid, stupid. But, he didn't say, or do, anything to retaliate, he simply went out the door. I was shocked. Not nearly as shocked as I was two minutes later when he turned on the garden hose and aimed it though the window at me, but none the less, shocked. Oh, and wet.

One of our classics was after we returned home from yet another drunken party. We had started to have words in the car on the way to the house. Something came up about him being married before. Once again, I blew it way out of proportion. I put the kids to bed while he also went on to bed. That wasn't working for me. I wanted to "talk about it". He was having no part of it, and told me to leave him alone. He rolled over with his back to me. I pushed him…. hard. As he turned back toward me, I lunged at him. I had some really deadly looking, long, fingernails. He brought his arm around to block my hands, and I lost my balance. I fell off the bed and hit the left side of my face on the baby bed that was beside ours. Then, I went the other way and hit the right side on our bedrail. I went to the bathroom crying, he followed to see if I was okay. Of course I wasn't, but now it was his time to leave me alone, and he did. The next morning, I had not one, but two black eyes. My brother, Don, picked a really bad day to stop by, what with the black eyes and all. For once, John saw his life flash before his eyes. I thought Don was going to kill him. I begged, he finally listened. I told him the truth, John had not laid a hand on me, I did it all by myself, with the help of The Miller Brewing Company. I'm not sure he ever believed me, but at least John lived.

I had many adventures with Don over the years. There were times when we argued as though we had known each other all our lives. It was always when we were drinking, and never too serious. Well, once he was so mad he fired me. I was working at his machine shop at the time, Don was a Class A Machinist. But he called the next morning and we worked it out. All I did was call him a male chauvinist pig. Come on, when he drank, he was. Okay, maybe it was a little harsh, but he knew exactly what to say to set me off.

But then, for my 24th birthday my big brother took Janelle, Linda, and I to Peru, Indiana with him. His band was playing at one of the bars, so we went along to listen. He had a good band, very good. As soon as he stepped on the stage he told every man in there to leave us alone, we were not only married, we were his sisters. He had sat us at the table closest to the stage, which was fine with the three of us, it looked like a rough crowd. One night a few weeks earlier, Don was playing there and a fight broke out. He tried to break it up, and was stabbed for his efforts. The guy was arrested and charged. The owners felt bad, so they were working harder at keeping the peace. We had so much fun. The three of us walked to the bathroom together, it felt safer, and we were trying not to draw attention to ourselves. On our way back to the table, Linda had this really long piece of toilet paper stuck to the heel of her shoe. She dragged that thing all the way through the bar-room. Don just shook his head. Class, we were nothing but class.

After he finished playing we headed east, back toward Huntington on Route 24. As we approached Wabash, Don saw Loretta Lynn's bus sitting at the motel, he was glad to see she was in town. Her mother lived in Wabash, I didn't know it until that night. He pulled in at the truck stop outside of Wabash for breakfast, by this time it was about 2 AM. Ironically, this truck stop was located at the intersection where the state police set up the roadblock to stop Dad and his Hudson that fateful night twenty years earlier. Anyway, we went inside and Don rushed over to a booth and was shaking hands with this guy and talking about how long it had been since they saw each other. Then I heard the man tell Don to go on over to his mom's house, that Loretta would be happy to see him. We finally sat down and Don told me that he was talking to J. Lee Webb, Loretta's brother. I'll admit I was impressed. Believe it or not, we finished our food and he drove to her Mom's house. He went to the door, knocked, and her Mom answered. He motioned for us to come in, so we did. I have to tell you I was shocked when Loretta came downstairs in a flannel shirt and jeans just to visit with us for a while. She was wonderful. We left her about 4 AM, and I was left with an unbelievable memory.

There was another night Don's band was playing in the Town of Andrews. John and I went to listen. Every time the band took a break, I went out in the alley with Don and had a shot of peppermint schnapps. It was really good. It was so good that I schnapped myself into one of the worst headaches ever known to man. His band played all over, and we tried to go as often as possible, but with John working nights it wasn't often. I always felt safe with Don, he was a big man, there weren't too many men that would mess with him. For me, he was a big huggable bear that loved me and called me "Sis". Don and Lou moved to Houston, Texas in 1980 after the death of their son, David. Don called me almost every Sunday afternoon until his death October 17, 1993. He was 54 years old when cancer took his life.

Back to the fateful parties of our youth. At one of the last parties John and I attended, came the final straw, along with the Huntington Police Department. A disturbed neighbor called and reported a disturbance, riot would have been a more fitting description. The usual people were there, along with a few other idiots. Everything seemed to be going well, at least the first hour or so. There had been a golf tournament that day that John, Jack and a guy named "Larry" had played in. (Larry isn't his real name, I decided to use it because I like neither him nor the last person I knew that had it.) The tournament was played at Etna Acres, the golf course where both the guys were members, and played all the time. They decided to leave the party and drive back out to the course to check the scores and see who won. They had finished their *rounds and left early that afternoon due to the party. There was really nothing wrong with this, but it would have been nice if they had told Linda and me that they were leaving. Larry had brought a girlfriend with him, and she, too, was left behind. Shortly before they drove off, a guy arrived in uniform. He was someone's brother and was home on leave from the Army. I don't know who he was, and it isn't relevant. It was then, I guess, but not now.*

The guys were gone about two hours, I guess they got lost, they had only lived in the county all their lives. Meanwhile, back at the ranch, the girlfriend of Larry was dancing with the military man, a lot. When the wayward golfers finally arrived back at the party, Larry saw his girlfriend dancing with the other guy through the huge picture window. He was furious, John and Jack were trying to calm him down before they came inside, they didn't want him fighting with a serviceman home on leave. Then for some unknown reason, this idiot (Larry) told John he shouldn't defend him because "your wife was dancing with him too". If John had been sober, he would have asked himself how Larry could have known this, unless he was Houdini. But no, that would make sense. The words went from Larry's drunken mouth to John's drunken ear, and that made it gospel. When the three of them came through the door it was pure chaos. Larry grabbed the poor guy dancing, and John grabbed me. The dancing guy was on the floor, I was pinned against the wall. Linda and I had spent our time in the kitchen talking. I'm sure it was the usual conversation about how our husbands were asses and all. I had not danced with anyone, nor did I know why he grabbed me, since he didn't ask first.

John still had me against the kitchen wall when we heard the sirens. Jack was trying to pull him away and talk to him, like that was going to work. He probably wouldn't have gotten so mad if I (in all my wisdom) hadn't said "it's really none of your business, you were the one that left", stupid, stupid, stupid. He pushed me out the back door and had me by the throat against someone's car in the driveway. By this time Jack was really pulling on him, telling him that Larry was lying. John let go just as the police came through the back door to see what the idiots in the driveway were doing.

Remarkably, there were no arrests. The owner of the house was the son of a detective on the force. We were lucky. Well, once I could breathe freely again, I felt pretty lucky. More good times.

All I can say is, if you find yourselves in these sorts of circumstances when you're "partying", it's not much of a party. Rethink your priorities, stay away from troublemakers, stay away from parties, and for God's sake, stay away from alcohol. See how easily that just flowed onto the paper? See how dull and boring that sounds? It's all in the hind site, and when you're young, you just don't have any.

In the meantime life went on. Neither of us stayed too upset after our little altercations, it wasn't worth it. Once you sober up, and get over the inevitable hangover, you see how silly all of it was. But, that Larry dude is still on my list. Enough for now about our blissful union. My sister once described the relationship between John and I as intense, little did she know.

Mom and Kathy were still doing well in San Francisco. Kathy had left DiMaggio's and was working elsewhere. Mom continued with her job, and was having fun with her new friends. They had both made a lot of new acquaintances, some better than others. She still attended cocktail parties, was still stubborn, and still a beautiful woman. Unfortunately for every man she met, she would never trust one again. Recently I was going through some of her things, I came across memorabilia she had saved from her years at DiMaggio's. Among these were menus, an ashtray, matchbooks, swizzle sticks shaped like little baseball bats with mitts attached to the top, and some newspaper articles. Two of the menu's had autographs. One was signed by Flip Wilson, he also wrote, "Ann, the devil made me do it". She was called Ann while she worked there. It fit on the badge much better than AnnaBelle. I can't make out the other autograph, I need to study it closer someday.

Then came the night that "AnnaBelle Meets the Hells Angels". There were times when Hell's Angels ruled Fisherman's Wharf. They would roll in, take over a bar, and generally destroy it before they were finished for the night. Talk about a party gone bad. There was little to nothing the authorities would do to stop them.

It seems impossible that a gang could hold that kind of power, but Hell's Angels did. I'm not sure why, but I don't believe they ever entered DiMaggio's; maybe they were baseball fans, who knows.

Two of Mom's friends owned a bar in San Francisco, and they were "hit" every so often. All her friends could do were to stand back and watch as their bar was destroyed. Hopefully, they had good insurance. One night, or early morning, Mom was waiting for her ride home after DiMaggio's had closed and her shift was over. She was evidently waiting on a taxi, a late taxi. She walked to a nearby phone booth, and was making a call to check on her ride when someone walked up behind and said, "you're coming with me mama". She told me later that; "Before I even turned around I said, I'm not going anywhere with you, you SOB, and I'm not your Mama". Evidently, in her anger, she hadn't heard the motorcycle pull up behind her. She said she turned around, saw the jacket before she saw the man, and almost passed out. For some unknown reason, he turned, got on his bike, and drove off, with about fifteen other jackets following him. He was lucky she didn't have her famous butcher knife. She was really lucky they didn't do anything to her. Maybe they weren't as bad as everyone thought they were back then. Or just maybe, he was tickled at this little woman with a huge attitude.

Mom moved back to Indiana in 1973. Her respiratory system began to weaken due to the dampness of the coast. As much as she hated to leave the city by the bay, it was time to go. She stayed at Monticello, Indiana with Granny for a short time. The two of them had always shared a closeness that was unmatched. I believe AnnaBelle was her favorite granddaughter. Perhaps because they were both small, industrious, determined women. Or, perhaps it was because AnnaBelle was Granny's first granddaughter, second to her brother Bud. These were Minnie's first two children, just as Minnie had been Granny's first born. Mom and Granny were both little women, in stature only. Their presence was huge, you could feel their energy.

Granny, born Martha Campbell, lived to be ninety-eight years old. She was born August seventh, eighteen and eighty-eight. I loved the way she said it. She saw so many changes in the world during her lifetime. Electricity came into every home, along with indoor plumbing. There was the automobile, airplanes, electric trains, toasters, microwaves, and disposable diapers. Her sons, and grandsons, served in World War II, the Korean War, and Vietnam. She was definitely one of a kind, and, along with AnnaBelle, one of the strongest willed women I have ever met. She, too, has been greatly missed by the entire family. I was blessed to be able to call her Granny.

It wasn't long before Mom made her way back to Indianapolis. In another bold move, she enrolled in Beauty College. This time, with determination, and drive behind her, she would finish school, pass the state board exam, and receive her license. After what seemed like an eternity, she would finally see her dreams become a reality. She suffered one major health setback while attending school that winter, she had to have surgery and they removed her gallbladder. At that time, it was a major surgery. I took the kids and went to Indy to stay with her for a few days after she was released from the hospital. This operation left her with a terrible infection at the sight of the incision, and a stone that they had missed. That stone would bother her for the rest of her life as it moved around in her system. These were very lean times for her. She was living in the dormitory located above the school, with very little money to survive on, but she made it. AnnaBelle was 47 years old when she completed The House Of James Beauty College course, and passed the state board exam to receive her license. She would never let them expire. This was her proudest achievement in life. (Not counting her daughters, she loved being our Mother, challenges and all.)

With her beauty license in hand, she accepted the position as manager at shop called "Beauty Care of Lawrence"; it was re-opening on the northeast side of the city, under new management. The address was 7207 East 46th Street, she loved the location. This was the perfect opportunity for her. She could do the cutting and styling she loved so much, yet not have to deal with the chemicals. All was right with the world again. She made good money, had a cute apartment, and even bought a little teacup poodle. Of course, she named her Fife. This was a big decision for Mom, she never allowed animals in the house when we were growing up, never. So Fife was one lucky little dog. I think Mom needed companionship, and this tiny dog gave her that and more. Fife lived 18 years and was Mom's one and only pet, ever. They traveled everywhere together.

I don't remember Mom dating while she was living back in Indianapolis. I strongly suspect Joe may have been there also. Our daughter Jenny would go for a visit with her Grandma every so often, loving every minute of it, and generally staying for a week. She would spend her days at the beauty shop with Mom. Naturally the patrons would spoil her, giving her things, buying her food. The shop was located in a mall with restaurants and stores.

On one of her visits to Indy, Jenny would meet the infamous Pal Horton. She still remembers the day she and her Grandma went to his house for a visit, probably because of the pool. She told me the one thing she never forgot was the wall of mirrors in the main room, and gold trim laced throughout the house. He had a beautiful home. There was a coffee table in the living room with a glass top. Under the glass were many pictures of movie stars with autographs that he and his parents had known. The Horton's were a very wealthy family, but Pal remained one of the most down-to-earth men I had ever met. Mom and Pal stayed in contact for years, he was the owner of Pal's Lounge. It had long since closed, his feelings for Mom had not. They would remain good friends, and nothing more. Unlike his many wives, (the ones with thin lips) Mom never took advantage of his generous nature. He was a sweetheart.

AnnaBelle remained in Indianapolis for about two years. Of course her greatest achievement was the completion of her schooling, but there was one more crowning glory she accomplished. She found the phone number and address of Jim Stovall, and in one short night made his life a living hell. She knew he was in Indiana, she soon learned he was living at Lafayette. The night she called his home, his current wife answered the phone. Mom introduced herself and then asked the woman if she had any children, she said yes. It seemed she had a teenage daughter. Mom started telling her to take her daughter and get away from him, or at least ask the girl if Stovall had ever done anything out of line. Jim could hear one side of the conversation and evidently didn't like it, he grabbed the phone and demanded to know who was calling. Mom had no problem telling him. She asked him if he had been messing around with this step-daughter too. He became furious, cussed her out, and hung up the phone.

Not to be deterred, she called back, this time the woman answered again, Jim was in the background yelling for his present wife to hang up the phone, but her curiosity was peaked, she wanted to talk to Mom. Being the AnnaBelle that she was, Mom had no problem complying with the woman's wishes. After quickly telling her what Stovall had done to the two step-daughters he claimed to love and care for so much, the wife wanted to know more. Finally, Stovall grabbed the phone, called Mom a bitch, and slammed it down. But, before he could hang up, Mom heard the woman start to ask him what the hell he did to those girls. Her job was done, she knew she had ruined his present marriage. Even though she had always wanted to cut his heart out with that famous butcher knife of hers, this would have to do, and it felt pretty good. She would always smile at this sweet memory. This is why you will never fool all the people all the time. There will forever be an AnnaBelle.

In time, AnnaBelle became bored with Indianapolis. She was ready to move on again. Although I'm sure she fought it, within a few months she left Indy and moved to Lowell, Indiana. This was where she had spent part of her young life with "Don", and ran her beloved "AnnaBelle's Restaurant". Here, in this small town not far from Valparaiso, lay many of the memories that would never leave her mind.

Her brother, Ray, lived at Lowell with his wife, Marie, and their children. He had moved from Culver shortly after the death of my Grandparents. He was the owner/operator of "Wicker Ford", one of the largest Ford dealerships in northern Indiana. He was very good at what he did. AnnaBelle and Ray had always been close, he was more than willing to help his sister. While living there, she joined the Moose, with the sponsorship of her brother, and once again had a social life. The two of them shared a love of entertaining and traveling, they did both on a grand scale. Her time spent at Lowell was happy. She took many trips with Ray and his family, she loved to travel. Well, there's a revelation.

I'm not sure why, but in 1976 AnnaBelle's next move was to Kankakee, Illinois, just south of Chicago. The only thing I can think of is that three of her four sisters were living in the area. All of her brothers and sisters were very close, she loved them so much. Don lived at Cedar Lake, Indiana, not far from the Illinois state line or the town of Lowell, where Ray lived.

Recently, among her many papers, I found her Illinois State Beauty License. I wasn't aware that she had gotten them. This lady is still full of surprises. I will never cease to be proud of all she accomplished, and how hard she fought to do so.

AnnaBelle continued to travel with her brother Ray on occasion. She did however make one trip to Florida by herself. She flew into Tampa to spend a few days with her brother James and his family. They lived close to St. Petersburg. While there, she suffered a mild heart attack, she was 51 years old, the year was 1978. When she was well enough to travel, she flew to Indianapolis where John and I picked her up at the airport and brought her to our house for a few days. We had just bought our first home, after renting for years, and were getting settled in.

When Mom felt strong enough to take care of herself, we took her back to Kankakee. She would never really be able to work again, not as she had in the past. It wasn't just her heart that would change her way of life, it was the weakness of her respiratory system as well. She never regained her former strength. Unfortunately, at that time, I didn't realize the impact this would have on her life. And in the end, my own.

It was at this time that Kathy decided to move from San Francisco to Kankakee and live with Mom. This was not a smart move, they had never gotten along while living together. Loving, yes. Close, yes. Living together, no. It didn't last long, Kathy went back to the west coast. She loved it out there, it was where she needed to be. Mom was better off living alone; she had become accustomed to her way of life. She would change her address at the drop of a hat, but not her independence.

AnnaBelle and Mr. John   1975
Mr. John was her hair stylist for shows.

AnnaBelle and Mr. John   1975
Another hair show.

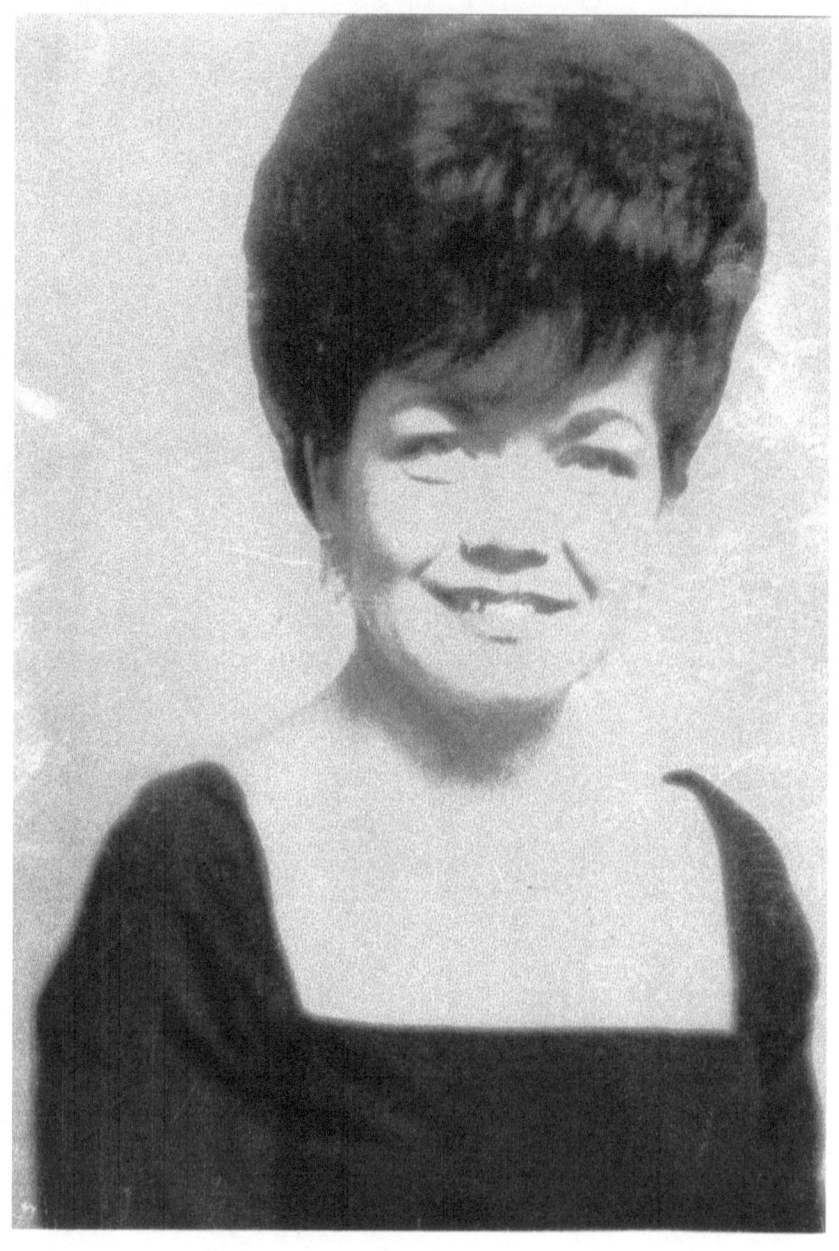

AnnaBelle   1976

Chapter X

INHERITING ANNABELLE'S SPIRIT

It was during this same time that John and I were standing completely still in our marriage. It was July 16, 1976 that started the changes in my life that I had been waiting for. Although some of the following has already been told, I feel the need to add to the story. It will always be the story without an end anyway, at least for me.

I finally felt comfortable working outside the home. I had been working for my brother, Don, at his machine shop, as his only employee. The shop suffered the effects of a fire, and needed extensive repairs that would take some time. Don decided to lay me off so that I could draw un-employment. I had to be actively seeking work, so I filled out an application for Utrad, never thinking they would hire me. But they did. I had not worked with the public since I was a teenager, which seemed a lifetime away. This was no drive-in, or department store, it was factory work. I was terrified, but I accepted the job, and started the next day, July 16, 1976. I worked from 4PM to 12:30PM. The hours were fine; John was working days and would be home with the kids at night. I didn't want to take the kids to a sitter, but for some strange reason, I wanted to accept this job. And in the end, I did.

My first night at work consisted of training amid chaos, there's just no other way to put it. I started in the inspection department, where they were short three inspectors at the time. The first two people I met were Jean, a wonderful, kind woman, and Tim, he was young and busy. There was no instant connection to Tim, that took a few months. But eventually, our relationship grew into one that was more than casual. It was destined to happen, the stars lined up, and there we were. Not surprising to me, but an un-expected turn of events for John. I'm still amazed that he say's he never saw it coming. At least until my actions came to light.

As I have said before, no one was more surprised than I was at his reaction to the news that I was seeing someone else, and planning to leave him. I didn't think he'd miss me until something wasn't done around the house. Like supper, laundry, cleaning, sex. Oh, come on, every woman in the world has felt the same at least once in their married life. In your heart, you know I'm right. I wasn't right about John in the end, but I was right in my feelings. He knew exactly why it had happened, he admitted that. But what he couldn't believe was that I would ever do it. I had told him for years something was going to happen, I couldn't sit and wait forever for the one thing that he found the hardest to give, a little of himself. I think men back then thought it was a sign of weakness. Yes, it's important to look manly in front of all the other guys, all the way to divorce court. Idiots.

My relationship with Tim started as a simple flirtation, mixed in with friendship. Just as I'm sure thousands of other have also began. He made me feel safe, secure, and interesting. That was the secret, when I talked, he listened, when he talked, I listened. I loved our conversations, and found I looked forward to them every night. I begin to dread the weekend, I missed him when I was home. I knew I was approaching dangerous territory with him, but it never occurred to me that he would feel the same. We started to go for rides after work. We both enjoyed the same music, the same foods, and each others company. I truly loved being with him. I knew what I was doing, and feeling, was so very wrong. I knew it then, just as I know it now. I simply didn't have the will to stop the madness before it went any farther.

However, it wasn't long before I realized he was serious. I still can't believe how much he loved me. I didn't believe him for a long time, I didn't understand why he wanted to continue with something that would profoundly change his way of life. He would be put into a family situation with the added responsibility of children, John's children. But then, when everything came out in the open, he was there for me. He told me he would do whatever I wanted him to. He would never leave me, not unless I told him it was over. It wasn't, and I couldn't. I had John on one side, begging me to stay with him. Tim on the other, willing to do whatever was needed to make my life easier. There was nothing left for me to do but move forward with my plans to leave John. I was about to find out it would be easier said than done. I was torn. Remember the song I mentioned before, "Torn Between Two Lover's"? It was released just in time for me to set and cry about.

Deep in my heart, I would always love John. There was something about him that still caused my heart to ache. I felt I had given him all I had to offer. No one, including Tim would ever have the part of me I gave to John. I wouldn't allow it a second time, plus, it no longer existed. But I had to keep things in perspective. I simply couldn't weaken. I felt, and still do, that if you love someone, you would never do anything to cause them pain or heartache. Ironic, isn't it. That's exactly what I was doing to John. Even though I came to realize that perhaps he did need me in his life, I also knew that I had no idea what he would do if I stayed with him. Would my life go back to the same old crap? Or maybe move on to some kind of new crap? Um, decisions, decisions.

After John found out about Tim, our time together was limited, just as it should have been, considering we shouldn't have been together at all. I missed our rides after work, the talks we used to have, and the fun, we actually had fun together. He gave me back my sense of humor; he watched over me, he took care of me. No one would ever mistreat me while I was with him; he had a strong presence about him.

That fateful Saturday that John and Tim met for the first, and only, time, will stay with me forever. Tim didn't hesitate to agree to the meeting when John asked. It brings things into perspective when your two worlds are standing face to face. Was there anyone or anything worth all this drama? After John left the house to meet Tim, I realized the gun was gone too. I honestly didn't know what he was capable of doing at that point. I knew them both; I knew they were both head-strong men. I also knew I could never live with the consequences if anything happened to either of them. It wasn't supposed to be this way. John was not supposed to care, he was not supposed to want me, and he was never supposed to fight *for me. I had told myself all along that John would be fine, better off really. Who needs a woman that never seemed to be happy? Let her go be a problem for someone else. Evidently, it wasn't going to be that easy. But life went on; none of us could stop that. I have to wonder myself if I'm trying to justify my actions by explaining his. Perhaps.*

After my filing for divorce, John buying the new wedding rings, the blizzard of 1978, Tim's wreck, John's wreck, "the burden", and eventually, our reconciliation, I was mentally exhausted. I am now, just writing that sentence. It was a long two years. It was also the two years that changed my life forever, and the lives of many others. The burden came in the form of a phone call the beginning of April, around 2 AM one morning. It was from Jack, the husband of my friend Linda, they had been like family to us for years, he and John were best friends. He said God came to him in a dream and told him that since I couldn't make up my mind, the decision would be taken out of my hands. Jack and I have never mentioned the phone call during the past 35 years. I have to wonder if he even remembers it, I'll have to ask him someday. I know I talked about this before, but it was such a profound moment in my life that I felt it was worth repeating.

Tim had a motorcycle wreck around April 11, 1978. I believe that was the date, strange, I can't remember exactly. I do remember it ended any hope of a future life with him, if that would have been the case. Within a week, on April 16, 1978, John was also involved in a wreck. He hit a tree head on, totaled his car, sustained broken ribs, and various bruises. Which could also have ended any life I may have had with him? He faired better than Tim however, Tim was in a coma, John spent two days in the hospital.

I won't go into great detail again, I just need to say that any decision I thought I had to make about the two men in my life was taken out of my hands. Tim stayed in a coma for weeks and when he awoke, it was obvious he had been left with brain damage. The doctors said it could take up to five years of therapy for him to show improvement, he would be right. At the end of those five years, my world would be turned upside down again. And that's the way it has stayed.

I have also talked about my trip with John W. to see Tim on his 25th birthday in the first book. That was May 13, 1983, the five years that his doctor had talked about were past him now. I remember that visit so well, as I should, it was my last with Tim. I'm grateful that I had one last moment to be held in his arms, and feel the comfort that his strength gave me. I vividly remember the conversation I had with Tim the morning following my visit with him, the conversation when he asked me not to come to see him again. I knew even then that he was right, seeing me again was not in his best interest. I didn't know it would trigger memories, I didn't know the extent to which this would upset him, I simply didn't know. All I did know was that when he put his arms around me, I felt loved. What he knew was that it wasn't the right thing to do. I'm sure he felt that I was where I needed to be in my life. It was doubtful Tim would ever be able to work again, and if he did, it would still be years in the future. He knew John was a good provider, something he couldn't be right now. Funny, I can see it all now. I can see that all the things that never really mattered to me to begin with, were about to control my life, as well as Tim's.

I have also talked about "the box" that Tim gave me on my last visit with him. He had written my name on the top in scroll lettering, it had to have taken quite a while for him to do. But it proves to me that he knew we would see each other again. It was as though the box was waiting for me. There were many questions about the contents, I hadn't revealed anything about what the box held inside, I had never told anyone about it. I guess I didn't think it mattered, evidently, it did. Though most of it was personal, I will tell you about two of the items that I found inside. One was a key ring with my name on it, and another was a hundred dollar bill folded into a small square.. The key ring he carried with him before he had his accident, I knew that. He told me when he called the next morning that he wanted me to buy records with the money. Though I didn't want the money, or the records, I did as he asked. The first album I bought was "Against The Wind", by Bob Segar.

This was the song he played for John W. and me when we went to see him, we sat in his bedroom and listened to the words as he instructed us to do. He said this song described the way he felt. It still makes me sad, but I continue to play it to this day. The other things are still too personal, and I choose not to disclose them at this time. Maybe someday, but this isn't the time. I will treasure "the box" forever.

After seeing Tim in May, I can't say my actions improved any. I was however, living with the regret that I broke my promise to John about staying away from Tim. I was still going to the Bell Café, still having "fun" with my friends, and still taking chances. Two months later, in July, John and I had a bit of a falling out. Yes, another one. He had left to go to Michigan for the weekend. He said he was going fishing by himself. (Like I really believed that.)

On Saturday evening I went to the Bell to see if any of my friends were there. That's just silly, one of them was always there. Later that night someone got the bright idea to drive to the town of Markle and play shuffleboard. One of the local bars had a table, the Bell didn't. I loved to play so I agreed to go. For the first and only time, I broke my own rule, I left my car at the Bell and rode with the others. I would regret that move by the next morning. It was close to 1:30 AM when we left the bar to make our way back to Huntington, I ended up with one of the guys. I had known him for years, he had been a friend of my brother, Don's. He had dropped off the others, but wouldn't take me directly to my car, he wanted to stop by his house first, actually, it was his mother's house. He was going to yet another party, and needed to change his clothes and pick up the beer he had stored at home. Yes, he looked as though he needed another party. This was the very reason I always stayed with my car, I was in control. This is a perfect example of where I did not want to end up. Don't get me wrong, he was a nice guy. He was 35 years old, never been married, living with mom, no threat there. When we arrived, his mother was in the living room watching television, even though it was 2 AM. She was crippled and never slept well, therefore, she was usually up. I visited with her while he got ready. I'm sure that's why he wanted me there, to pacify his mom, she was always on him about his drinking.

It took what seemed like forever, but finally, he was ready to take me to pick up my car. He put the cooler full of beer in the front seat of his old truck, there was barely room for me squeeze in on the other side. (There's a reason I say that.) Off we went. The last thing his mother said to him was "be careful". He was awfully bad to drink, I know, like I should talk. Well, at that time anyway.

We drove across town, heading for the Bell Cafe, it was getting daylight by this time. We only lived three short blocks from the bar, so I wasn't far from home. As we neared the intersection at the last light before reaching my precious car, I noticed someone standing in the middle of the street. Actually he was in the middle of the intersection. My first thought was that it was some drunken fool. My second thought chilled me to the bone, it was none other than John standing there. Actually it was more of an omen than a thought. I said "Stop the truck". He said "Why". I said, "That's John". He turned pale, but he stopped. John walked over to the driver's side of the truck, I thought he was going to pull the guy out and kill him. The look on his face was really scary. He told me to get out of the truck and get my ass home. He told my ex-friend that if he ever saw him again, he would kill him. That was a little severe since he had the guy by several inches and forty pounds. I ended up walking to the house without my car. After all that, the waiting , the visiting, trying to be patient, wishing I had driven myself, I ended up without my car. There is no end to the madness.

Once we got to the house, the battle started. This was beyond a doubt the maddest I had ever seen him. The more we talked, the worse he became. He accused me of being all cuddled up with the guy and then moving over quickly when I saw him. I told him over, and over, there was a case of beer sitting on the seat between us. Now he wanted to know where he lived, he was going over there. I honestly couldn't have found my way back over there if I had to, I paid no attention to where it was. He didn't believe me, I finally told that even if I knew I wouldn't tell him, because of the mother. That made him even more angry, he thought that was an even bigger lie. There was no pleasing this man. Finally it was over. He told me to see a lawyer on Monday, and file for divorce, he was done.

Are you familiar with the movie, "The Perils of Pauline"? I felt I was living it. I absolutely couldn't blame John for being upset, he had every right to be. (Upset is an understatement.) I know I would have been just as upset as he was, possibly more. I wanted to remind him that he was the one who left me, AGAIN, to go on yet another fishing trip. That would have been a huge mistake. I knew to let that sleeping dog lay there.

It was a bad morning that quickly developed into the weekend from hell. I felt sorry for Johnny, he was only 14, so he was still stuck with us. I know this was very disturbing for him. He walked to the Bell with me Sunday morning so I could get my car and bring it home. Although it didn't really matter one way or another, the damage had been done.

I went to the lawyers and filed for divorce, one more time, on the following Monday. Thank God we lived in a different county, I would have been really embarrassed to re-file in the same place as before. That one had been dropped. This one was filed at the courthouse on July 21, 1983. Eventually, it too, would be dropped, but it took some time. It was days before we even spoke. If we hadn't still had one child at home, I don't know how it could have ended. Who am I kidding, for some strange reason, John and I seem to be destined to stay together. You could call it fate, that's not what I call it, but you could.

When I filed the second divorce action in July, it had been a little over two months since I had seen Tim on his birthday. In another five short weeks he would make he decision to take his own life. I feel certain he had heard the news, but I doubt he knew the reason why. And, I will never know if it had any bearing on his decision to end the situation once and for all. So, after all the turmoil of the last seven years, it ended. Tim was gone, John was relieved, we worked things out, and I didn't really understand any of it. But then, we rarely do.

Unbelievably, my life with John was basically back to where it had been before I met Tim. With one huge exception, now both of us had other things to do. I didn't like where my life was headed, but I didn't seem to have a better plan, so I just rolled with the flow. Again, the irony, now I didn't have either of them. Going to see Tim had been a lifeline, but for some reason, it was pulled away. I have to say, right or wrong, I know I would do it again.

My thoughts were out of control. Tim was still in my mind. I really needed to focus on something else, like life in general. What was I thinking? Why did I do the unthinkable? Why did he have the wreck? Why did he have to be left with the mind of a child? Would he have ever fully recovered? Could John and I ever really be happy? Can I stop with the questions? I get a little carried away at times.

When I think back over the years that changed my life, and the lives of so many others, I'm not sure I would change anything I did. I'm not sorry for my relationship with Tim, how could I be? It was the one time in my life I had honesty in a relationship. We had no reason to hide anything. We began the right way, as friends. Without him even knowing it, he forced me to think about what was important to me. I learned to believe in myself, and know my own strength. That remains with me. What I am sorry about is this; the pain it led to, and the loss it left in the hearts of many. Not everyone is capable of giving that much of themselves to another person. Tim did, and in the end, it was probably the biggest mistake he could have made. He lives in my heart, and there he will stay. I will never have that kind of relationship again in my life, nor do I want one. I am happy in knowing he loved me enough that he made sacrifices no other person has ever made for me. I am eternally grateful for his life, and, at the same time, eternally sad due to losing his presence here on earth. He may have taken his own life, but he has left a lifetime of memories for me. I will love him forever.

This may sound completely off any known wall, but my love for one, had nothing to do with my love for the other. I loved them for entirely different reasons. As I've said before, put the two of them *together, and it would have been the perfect man. I probably would never have met him, but he would have been perfect. I finally had to face the fact that John didn't feel the love I was expecting from him, because in the real world, it doesn't exist. It only exists in my mind, and the poetry I write. I am the dreamer, John is the realist. He keeps me grounded, whether I like it or not. Let's just say he tries.*

I know my train of though seems to travel in many directions, but, that's because I have so much to say. As with each of us, there are many actions and reactions that brought us to the point we are at in our lives. So please bear with me, and if at all possible, may someone learn something from the endless twists of circumstances. I know I have made some very poor choices during our marriage, but believe me, John has been between the rock and that hard place many times himself. I will explain two incidents that again took me to Pauline's place of perils. There isn't a shovel big enough to bury these with.

In 1976, while I was still working for Don at his machine shop, John and I had the occasion to go out with Don and his wife Lou one evening. Their son Kent was in a band and they were playing at a small bar in town, we went to listen to them. There was a teenaged girl singing in the band too, her parents joined us at our table. It was a pleasant enough evening, and the band was good. I really enjoyed listening to them. All's well that ends well. You'd think so anyway, wouldn't you?. The next morning at work, Lou and I were the only two in the shop working. She asked me if I knew who the other woman at our table was. I told her no. She said she was going to tell me, because she didn't think it was right that I sat there all night talking to her without knowing the truth. It was the woman who had written me the letter eleven years earlier about the child she had with John. I'm going to call the woman "Jean". It seems the girl singing was the child.

There is just no way to explain the many thought's that raced through my mind. But mainly, I loved my sister-in-law for at least respecting me enough to tell me, since obviously, no one else had. Thank God I had a few hours to cool down before I went home, it gave John a reprieve. When confronted about it, he asked me what I thought he should have done at that point. I told him I wouldn't have made him look like a complete fool by sitting there talking to her. It was the second time this woman had caused me grief, I wish I could say there wasn't another. Did he really think he was going to turn this around? It was never going to happen, neither of us was going to live that long, no human does. I ended up letting it go, on the outside.

It was about two months after this fiasco that I met Tim. This is not an excuse for what I did, it just explains my frame of mind. With this man there was no ex-wife, no secret babies anywhere, no leaving me sit in a car while he goes to a party, no fishing trips, and finally, he talked to me. I also knew that no one would ever hurt me without answering for it. This I knew for certain, it had already been demonstrated. So perhaps you can see why I may have been a little torn.

About ten years after the band incident, I had another "awakening". There were quite a few of us from work that regularly went for a drink at the end of our shift. The Bell Café was across the street, so it wasn't far to go. There was one particular lady that I found to be fun. She loved to laugh and have a good time. One Friday evening she told me one of her friends was going to meet us after work for a drink, this friend wanted to meet me. I guess she and this lady had been close for years. I said fine. That particular night, John and his friend, Kenny, were going to meet me there too. John would come over every so often on a Friday night and have a beer with me, he always knew where I was. The lady from work introduced me to her friend, and insisted I sit with them for a while, and I did. John was unusually attentive, bringing me a drink when mine was empty. This alone should have sent up big red flags, huge red waving flags. John never waited on me, it wasn't in his nature. I probably sat talking with the women about two hours, then John, Kenny and I went out for breakfast. Where were the flags???

The very next morning I went back to the Bell to work in the kitchen for a couple of hours. I guess I was there so often Steve, the owner, decided to put me to work. That's not really true, I did help out occasionally though, he trusted me, we had been friends for years. The bartender on duty the next morning just happened to be that freak "Larry", the one from the party years earlier who had almost gotten me killed by John. He had also been there working the night before. Eventually, he called me over to the bar and asked me how "Jean" was doing. I told him I had no idea, I didn't even know her. He said "Well, that's odd, you sat there and talked to her for two hours last night." Even now I find it's hard to breathe when I think about it. I truly thought my head was going to explode. Can that really happen? I was pretty sure it was about to. Have you ever heard the expression dumb-founded? It happens, I was struck dumb, without speech, unable to talk, barely breathing. I don't remember a time that I was as angry as I was that day, ever.

Unfortunately for John, it was Saturday, he wasn't fishing, he was home, and I'm sure he was still praying that I would never find out who I had been talking to the night before. He wasn't on his knee's, but I'm sure there was still praying going on. Of course all hope went out the window when I walked in the door and called him the "bastard" that he truly was. And then, he had the gall, we'll use gall, to again ask me what he was supposed to do. I was the one that walked over to her table, sat down and carried on a conversation with her. I won't even bother to write the remainder of the conversation we had that day. Let's just say it got ugly, really ugly. The language was very bad, and I want this book to be able to be entered into the public library someday. You know the worst part of this entire mess? I didn't remember her face then, and I wouldn't know her if I passed her on the street today. God, how I hate that, I could still be talking to her. I should have just shot him the first time. No not that time, the letter and the being in the car time. The idiot. Well, at any rate, one of us is an idiot. I swear, if he was awake right now, I could just smack the crap out of him. More good times, again.

Now, back to the story, or, meanwhile, back at the ranch. After buying the house and moving into Huntington, we found we were still both working long, hard hours. John worked days, I was still on second shift. We didn't see each other very often. It wasn't the way to mend a marriage, but it was the way to have things in life. He bought a beautiful bass boat and joined Indiana Bassmasters, I bought new clothes and joined my friends at the Bell Café for a drink after work. It never occurred to me that Mom may be having a rough time of it. I guess I was used to her taking care of herself, and the spirit of strength she had always carried with her.

John and I had been married for 21 years in 1986 when he was diagnosed with cancer. After two surgeries and weeks of recovery, it was determined he was in stage 3. He had the maximum of 36 radiation treatments on both sides of his neck and chest. It was a battle he fought and won. We knew how lucky we were, we had both watched members of our families lose the fight. God was watching over him, and took care of him. Evidently, our time together was still not finished. Since that time John has gone through seven other major surgeries. He is a strong man, and seldom complains. So you can see why I have to. It's a nasty job, one of those that somebody has to do.

AnnaBelle   1977
Going Blonde

Top: Carolyn Sue, John, Kathy, AnnaBelle
Bottom: Johnny and Jenny
Family Reunion, Monticello, In. August 1978

AnnaBelle and Carolyn Sue
Family Reunion   August 1978

Chapter XI

ANNABELLE & ME...... TOGETHER AGAIN

When do you reach the point in life where the roles of parent and child begin to reverse? More importantly, how do you know? I certainly didn't have a guidebook, nor does anyone. We never want to face the fact that our parents may not remain the strong, independent people they have always been to us. We know they will always worry about us. Then suddenly one day, we find ourselves worrying more about them. Slowly the transformation starts, the child becomes the caregiver.

My Uncle Ray called me on a Friday night to let me know what a terrible daughter I was by not looking after my Mother. He had me in tears before he was done with his ranting. He was right in what he was saying about her needing help, but wrong in his approach to me. When I had spoken to Mom on the phone, I never suspected she was having a hard time. She never let on, and of course, she wouldn't. She didn't have a job, she didn't have enough to eat, she didn't have transportation, she didn't have insurance, but most of all, she didn't have a daughter taking care of things for her. At least, according to Uncle Ray this was how it looked. It would be years before I told her about that phone call, and then only after I received another call, from yet another brother. And well after Uncle Ray had passed away, he was safe.

Uncle Ray and I finally decided that I would go get Mom, bring her for a visit, talk her into moving closer, find her a place to live, and then move her to Huntington. He said he would pay the moving expenses and help in any way he could. In the end, I did what I said I would, and he made arrangements for the truck and the move. I found I worried constantly about her now, if only I had known before. She was a very proud, very stubborn woman. I guess she thought I had enough going on in my life. Of course it could have been that she would have rather lived anywhere besides

Huntington. She had never been wild about the town. That would not change.

Things were much better after Mom moved to Huntington. I no longer had to worry about what she was doing, all I had to do was help her take care of business. It wasn't long before her finances, insurance and health began to improve. She was finally back on track, which was where AnnaBelle had to be to in order to be happy. We had always gotten along very well, that would never change. I really loved having her near. We had dinners, went shopping, and I found the holidays were more fun with her living close by. We had always enjoyed the same things, and could talk endlessly, for hours, on the phone.

My life did take on more meaning while Mom lived in Huntington, though I never realized or appreciated it at the time. We went on trips together, something John and I seldom did. Mom and I went to McArthur, Ohio for four days to visit relatives, and to reminisce about times gone by. Mom's uncle, Jerry Griffith (My Great-uncle, naturally.) lived there with his wife, Aunt Ella, as he had done for years. He was Grandma's brother, and one of the kindest men I have ever met. He was not only the minister of the Free Will Baptist Church that he, himself, had built, but president of the one and only bank in town.

The drive to McArthur was uneventful, we stopped to have lunch with Mom's brother, Harold, on our way there. He lived close to Columbus, it was good too see him and his daughter that day. His wife was working and couldn't join us. We arrived in McArthur at dusk, drove straight to the one and only motel in town. I had made reservations the week before. This town was really off the beaten path, I couldn't understand why I had to have reservations, but when I called to see if they were still open, I found I did. She said they had only two rooms available for the weekend we would be there, I reserved them both. We would find out why they were so busy the first morning there, when we ventured out of our rooms. Of all the people in this world, after living with John, I should have known it was hunting season.

Uncle Jerry had wanted us to stay with them, but Mom and I decided we would rather have our own rooms where we could come and go as we pleased, without bothering anyone. He came to the motel as soon as we had called to let them know we made it to town. He came to my room first, Mom's was next door. I assured him we were comfortable, settled in, and would see them first thing in the morning. The lady at the motel had forgotten to turn the heat on in the rooms before our arrival, and it was freezing. It did eventually warm up, right before we checked out three days later. Again, the "No Tell, Motel" comes to mind. Anyway, he wanted to see Mom, so I took him next door. As I live and breathe, she was sitting on the bed wearing flannel pajamas, a bathrobe, huge furry slippers and a parka with the hood pulled up over her head. Oh, and gloves, can't forget the gloves. She looked like Nanook of the great north. I had just told Uncle Jerry we were fine, I lied to a minister….. Great.

He stayed until it began to warm up a little and then reluctantly went home without us, he knew we would see him early the next morning for breakfast. I, too, ended up wearing everything in my suitcase to bed. Unfortunately, shortly after Uncle Jerry left us, there was a power outage. It was off about two hours, now we're talking cold, and dark, very, very dark. I got out of that half-way warm bed when the lady that managed the place knocked on the door and handed me a flashlight. I decided that since I was already up, I would go next door and check on Mom. The only part of her that was visible were those blue eyes peaking out of the covers. They spoke volumes. They very clearly said, "Yes Carolyn Sue, let's go to Ohio, perhaps a God forsaken McArthur, Ohio. And, by all means, let us stay at the No-tell Motel. You know, the one with no heat, uncomfortable beds, and lets make sure it has a bunch of nasty deer hunters staying there too. Yes, lets do that." This was one journey she could have lived without, but we did end up having fun.

The next morning I got up and tried to take a quick shower, and I mean quick, God it was cold. Well, I guess it usually is in November. I dressed quickly, and went to the office and got a cup *of coffee for Mom. I knew when I knocked on her door I best have some kind of peace offering, coffee was a sure thing. In a perfect world, there would have been biscuits; she loved breads in any form. I swear, I would have baked them myself, if I had an oven. My kingdom for an oven…and heat, just a little heat.*

She finally got out of that one and only warm spot in her room and dressed A.S.A.P. I just couldn't figure out how to tell her about the dead deer hanging in the tree out front, gutted and all. The only thing to do was pray she wouldn't notice it. If only that would have happened. I'm telling you, those eyes of hers could bore holes into your very soul. It ended up being a good year for the hunters, every morning there were two or three fresh deer hanging in the trees. It was like something from the X-Files.

Our second trip together was to a place called Little Nashville, located in southern Indiana. It's a wonderful little town full of shops that sell everything you could possibly want to buy on a Christmas shopping trip. We went in November, the town was completely decorated for the holidays. It was beautiful, and very old fashioned. We stayed for three days, lodging at The Hampton Inn , a far cry from our first trip. I would recommend this little Christmas Village for anyone who likes to take a step back in time. Did I say they had candy shops? Oh, they did. Fudge, yummy, yummy walnut fudge.

There came a time when we also took a short, four day trip, to Valparaiso. Mary J. would join us for this little excursion. Again, we shopped, we ate, and had fun. "The Chili Bowl", located just outside Valpo on Highway 30 is "the" place to eat. If you're ever in the area I seriously suggest you stop there for a meal. The place has been there forever, because the food is excellent. We ventured to Merrillville to see Wayne Newton in concert on that Saturday night, he really puts on a good show. Everyone acted like we were going to see Peter Pan, I swear, some people. We spent that Friday at the courthouse, in the attic (it seemed like an attic), going through huge ledgers with marriage records in them. We were trying to find out when and where Mom and Jim Stovall were married. She was pretty sure they were married at Valpo (Porter County), she was pretty sure it was 1952, she was pretty sure she was there. We were positive she didn't remember anything for sure. I asked her how she could forget. She said if you really wanted to, you could forget anything. We found nothing pertinent while we were there, and we were pretty sure we wouldn't. Okay, I'll stop.

We needed the necessary information about Stovall because we had learned that Mom could draw from his social security, which would double her benefits. In my mind, he may finally be useful for something. In her mind, it would be her final revenge. But first, we had to have the proof that they were married for the required ten years. That wouldn't be an easy task, but nothing for AnnaBelle was ever easy. After hiring a detective and a lawyer, we finally retrieved all the information we needed to go forth. I'm going to add this as a learning experience. Keep records, and always check your options. In the end, they were not married in Valparaiso, Porter County in 1952. The ceremony took place in Rensselaer, Jasper County, on June 13, 1953.

Stovall left our lives in Florida, May, 1961. Because he could not be found, (There was that nasty little arrest warrant hanging over his head.) Mom never legally divorced him, I guess she just forgot it ever happened. She didn't remarried, so it never became an issue. In the end we found out that she was, indeed, divorced. Evidently Stovall filed here in Indiana after the one year waiting period. (We all knew he had returned to the home of his parents.) It was called "divorced by default", and was granted to him on June 22, 1962. This left her short by one of the ten required years. I'm sure he was smart enough to have known this may happen, and wanted to stop her from having a claim on his benefits. Evidently, he didn't remember the real AnnaBelle, and the tenacity that drove her. In reality, truth be told, Mom and Jim Stovall had "lived together, in sin", for fourteen months prior to their wedding ceremony. (Bad Mommy.) No, they had not been legally married for the necessary ten years for her to draw from his social security, but common law marriage was recognized and deemed legal until January 1, 1958 in the state of Indiana. However, proving it was going to pose a bit of a problem.

Twenty four years had passed since my last trip to Uncle Shep and Aunt Gatha's house. (Shep was Jim Stovall's brother.). That was in 1968 for a pheasant hunting trip when I traveled to their farm with John. She was the only person I knew to call for help. Above all, we needed Stovall's social security number to proceed with our efforts in enabling Mom to receive his benefits. I thought perhaps she could get it for me, without us having to face him. And then, miracle of miracles, she informed me of his death six years earlier on April 15, 1985. She said he died a terrible, painful death, suffering with stomach cancer. Now I know I should have felt bad. But instead, I hung up the phone, called Mom, and began to sing, "Ding Dong the witch is dead, witch old witch, the wicked witch". I don't think I'll be severely punished for that, I simply lost my head and was caught up in the moment. Come on, you know it was the right thing to do. In the end, we didn't need his number, all she had to do was report his death. Which she gladly did. Ironically Stovall died on Dad's birthday, April 15th. It would have been the best present ever. It may have been anyway, I hope Dad was waiting on him..... With a real bad attitude.

The only way to prove that they had "lived together, in sin" for those first fourteen months was to obtain affidavits from people who new them at that time, and would be willing to sign notarized statements to that affect. I believe she needed a total of five witnesses. Since the terms of their break-up were not anything a family wanted to dwell on, she didn't think his family would be of much help, and these were the people she needed the most. In the end, they evidently didn't like him either, three of them filled out the paperwork and returned it to her, signed and notarized. The one that bore the most weight with the judge was from his sister, Ethel. All I can say is bless her.

That was the only good thing he ever did for her, it doubled her benefits. After her phone call to his wife, I'm sure he was spinning in his grave at the thought of helping her at all. I had spoken to him once in all the years since last seeing him in St Pete. That phone call never should have happened. I regret I even took the *call, circumstances kept me from making a scene. The year was 1968.*

Let me clear up the 1968 hunting trip. As I've said before, John loved to hunt. He pheasant hunted in the area around Huntington, but the birds were elusive and scarce. He had mentioned the best place for pheasant was in western Indiana close to the Illinois state line. I knew Aunt Gatha and Uncle Shep had a farm south of Boswell, in the same area. Since they were always good to Kathy and I, never approving of the way his brother treated us, I felt comfortable in calling them. They said John could absolutely come and hunt their property, but they wanted me to come too. So, I went, at least the on first trip they made. I did have a wonderful day visiting with them. They had promised not to tell Jim Stovall anything about me coming, he was living at Lafayette. By this time Mrs. Stovall, Jim's mother was very elderly, and living with Shep and Gatha. Unfortunately, she let her evil son know I was going to be there. Of course he called as soon as he got home from work that afternoon, and said he could be there in a half hour. The only reason I spoke with him was because his elderly mother was sitting right there, and I wouldn't upset her for anything. I told him we were just leaving. Jim Stovall showing up at the same location as John Morris with a loaded gun would never end well. He had the nerve to foolishly asked me, "Do you think your Mother would see me?" I told him "no". Of course, I'm sure after her phone call to his wife a few years later, he wanted to do more than see her.

When I told Mom about talking to him, she said she would love to see him; she would be waiting for him.....with a butcher knife. She wanted to stab him in the heart when she opened the door. Such a sweet demeanor, never expressing her true feelings, never holding a grudge, wouldn't hurt a fly. All these things and so many more, were never my AnnaBelle.

While living in Huntington, Mom moved five times. Which wasn't really too bad for eleven years. The last place she rented was a little house on Greenacre Drive. It was perfect for her. This was the period of time that she devoted herself to the care of Kassandra (Kassie), and Rachel. These two little girls were her first Great-

granddaughters, and the loves of her life. She was in her element, caring once again for "the girls". To this day, their Grandma Bollan holds a special place in their hearts. As they got older, she was the one person they made sure they still spent time with, no matter where she was living.

She had lived on Greenacre Drive in Huntington for about two years when she decided to move to Manteno, Illinois and live close to her sisters again. Things didn't work out as well as expected in Manteno, not a big surprise to me. So after about a year, she moved back to Indiana, ending up in Valparaiso, almost coming full circle.

While she lived in Valpo, I would go visit her often. This was a rough time for her. Communication with her sisters had broken down, as it will in any family from time to time. She refused to go to the famous Wicker Family Reunion that year because no one had bothered to call and see if she had a way there and back home. I hadn't planned on attending that year. I was working ten hour days, six days a week, in the auditing department at the factory. But, due to Mom being upset, I got up that Sunday morning and drove to Valpo, determined that she should go. She was just as determined that she wasn't. This was just wrong, she lived for her family reunions, absolutely loving them. When I got to her apartment, she had prepared the food that they all loved so much, including her cherry delight. I still don't know how they could ignore her that way, but they did. They didn't even live that far from her. I finally got her and the food in the truck, and drove to Cedar Lake, where it was being held. She would not get out of the vehicle. Did I say she was stubborn??? In the end, one of her favorite nephews (they were all her favorites), "Wick", talked her out of the truck and into the pavilion. She was still unhappy, but she went, broken heart and all.

I enjoyed my visits to Valparaiso while Mom lived there. I would go for the weekend, we would have fun. We shopped, ate out, explored the town, and reminisced about times gone by. One weekend we went to the theater to see "Sleepless In Seattle", what a good movie. It was a typical chick flick, one that we both loved.

It was released shortly before Christmas that year, perfect timing. Downtown Valpo hadn't changed all that much in the 35 years since we had left it. They still played Christmas music in the town square, and there was the hot dog wagon on the corner. It brought back memories of my childhood, the good memories. I treasure the time I was allowed to spend with Mom in the town that meant so much to both of us.

Chapter XII

AnnaBelle's Spirit Comes Full Circle

The Angel Finds Her Wings

AnnaBelle remained in Valparaiso about a year. At this time, her brother Jim, who lived in Florida, was talking to her regularly. He lived in the St Petersburg area. He was a realtor, and had found a mobile home that would be perfect for her. The home was located in a nice park at Largo. Within a couple of months, she made arrangements to purchase the home, packed her belongings, and made her plans to move to Florida once again. Kathy flew to Chicago's O'Hare Airport where Aunt Barb's husband, Bob, picked her up and took her to Valpo. She would be the one to drive the rental truck, loaded with all of Mom's possessions, to her new home in Florida. Now, AnnaBelle had come full circle.

They drove to Huntington and spent one night at our house before heading out. Mom was concerned about being so far from me, but I knew how badly she wanted to go, and I told her I could be on a flight and down there within a few hours. And so it was, for the next thirteen years, I would take my vacations and fly to Florida to see Mom. I went two to three times a year, sometimes more. Each summer, she would fly to Indiana and spend 4 to 6 weeks with us. One of John's favorite memories was the way she would cuss at the politicians she constantly watched on the television. I didn't know how bad she was until one day when I got on him about his cussing while the three of us were eating supper. He looked at me and said, "Me? You should hear her back in that bedroom when you're not here". She just smiled when I turned to look at her. John and I both loved having her, she and I loved every minute we spent together. During this time she would always attend the family reunion, usually held in Illinois. There *would never be a repeat of the Valparaiso fiasco. Her brothers and sisters always remained close.*

During the thirteen years that Mom lived in Florida, I talked to her no less than twice daily. Thank God for the unlimited long distance that had come to pass. I would have had to acquire a second job if not. I missed having her near; there were times that I begged her to come back. But, knowing how much her health had improved with the warmer climate, I knew that would never happen. I don't think she could have survived another winter in Indiana. The year was 1994, I think it was very gutsy to make that major of a move at 67 years of age. AnnaBelle never lacked for the thrill of a new adventure, at any age. I loved her sense of adventure, her drive, and her ability to make the best of almost any situation.

Mom had lived in Florida about a year when Kathy made the move to join her. I was hoping it was the right thing, for both of them. But of course, my thoughts were mainly on Mom. With Mom, her thoughts were on her daughter at the time. Kathy wasn't doing well in San Francisco, Mom was the one who asked her to come and live with her. For the first time in many years, it was AnnaBelle who was doing well. It didn't take long for Kathy to find a job with Publix. She would work her way from cashier to Administrative Coordinator in a short period of time.

Eventually, Mom would sell her little mobile home in Largo, she and Kathy moved to Clearwater Beach. They found a nice, two bedroom apartment located on Brightwater Drive, close to the beach. The screened-in porch overlooked the water, it was perfect. Mom had wanted to move out by the beaches for some time. They lived there for about five years. That was pretty much a record for AnnaBelle, although every weekend she scoured the Sunday classified ads for apartment and condos. That restless spirit would eventually get the best of her.

The next move for Mom and Kathy was to a condo on St Pete Beach. They rented a place on the ninth floor, overlooking the water. The view was beautiful. I was surprised that Mom would live on the ninth floor, until I saw the view, it spoke volumes. It was here that the relationship between the two of them became quite strained, and began to break down. I will not go into details, there is no need, and, it is not what Mom would want me to do. Finally Mom decided to find a place of her own. It was time for the two of them to live separately. Although painful, it was necessary at the time.

It just so happened that one of Mom's sisters had recently moved to St Pete Beach herself and bought a condo at Bay Island Estates. There were rentals available within the complex. Ironically, there was a one bedroom condo for rent at the time. Mom leased it immediately. It was located on the fourth floor of a building across from my aunt's, again overlooking the water, and was perfect for Mom. There were four pools located on the property, it was wonderful. But, most importantly, there was a private bridge that led across the water to the doctor's offices and hospital. She would live in this apartment for three years. I, too, loved the place. It was gated and secure, I knew she was safe. There was a guard on duty 24/7.

Mom had lived at Bay Island for about a year when Kathy would follow her there. She too rented a condo, in yet another building. Hers was located on the first floor. This arrangement worked out quite well, they were close, yet separate. This is the way it stayed for the next two years.

I was flying to Florida two to three times a year and staying for a week to ten days. Usually I would rent a car, Kathy needed hers for work, and it was just easier. Mom and I would spend the days out and about as much as possible. We would shop, have lunch, and shop some more. We always bought silly little things that neither of us really needed, but those are the most fun. Of course, then I had to worry about getting the stuff home. There were times I actually had to pack the items and ship them.

Over the years, there were times when I would make an emergency flight, due to Mom's health. The year 2003 brought one of the worst scares of my life. I just returned home from a trip to Florida, I hadn't even completely unpacked my suitcase yet. The morning after my arrival back in Huntington, I called Mom to check *in with her. Kathy was getting ready to take her to the hospital; she had been having more trouble than usual with her breathing. About an hour later I called the hospital to see how she was doing. I talked to Mom in the emergency department; they were getting ready to take her for a c-scan. Although she had never had one before, none of us were too worried. I waited for a return call from Kathy to let me know how it went. I finally became impatient and called the hospital myself. The operator said she couldn't put the call through to emergency; they had a code blue in place.*

My first reaction was this sinking feeling. I knew it was Mom. I can't begin to describe the fear. My heart pounded, I found I was having difficulty breathing, I thought I was going to pass out. I waited for what seemed like hours, finally Kathy called. Mom had gone into cardiac arrest and was now on complete life support. Kathy was beside herself, I was of no help to her. I remember not knowing what to do first. Strangely, I went out to the barn and started to pace in circles. I couldn't seem to breathe, God, how I wanted this to not be happening. John called the kids to come over; he had no idea what to do with me. At that point, no one could do anything. I did learn one thing that day, there is no way you can foresee how you will react to any given situation. I finally came to my senses, called the airline and booked a flight back to St Petersburg. It was early the next morning before they could get me on a flight, the longest flight of my life. (That's what I thought at the time anyway.)

The flight itself took about two hours. In those two hours my mind went from present to past and back again. I prayed, I begged God to please be with her, please help her to overcome this. The one thing I remember clearly was hearing the song "Run For The Roses"; it's about horses and racing. Mom loved the bluegrass hills of Kentucky, the horses, and she loved to attend the Kentucky Derby. But, the song also fit her, and her life. This is the point where you know you have to face the reality that you may lose this person; I found there was no point at which I could. As much as I loved her, I never appreciated what a huge part of my life she was. For the entire flight the tears never left my eyes, they never overflowed, but never left. My God, how I loved this little woman named AnnaBelle.

The plane landed in Tampa, I took a shuttle from the airport to the hospital at St. Pete Beach. For once the erratic driving across Tampa Bay didn't bother me. When I arrived at the entrance, Kathy was standing there waiting on me. She took me to Critical Care, one place I had never been. Intensive Care, yes, but Critical Care, I didn't even know it existed. They had called in a special nurse for Mom, her name was Lee. I met her first; she took me to Mom's room. You can never be prepared for what awaits you there, nor was I. She looked so tiny, lying there so still. She was in a coma; her little hands were tied to the railings. There were machines and tubes and needles everywhere. Again, I was having difficulty breathing; Lee assured me Mom could feel nothing. How could she not feel the two tubes going down her throat, the one in her nose, and the needles in her arms and chest? How could this be?

We were only allowed in her room for a short period of time every two hours. Lee was very strict, but I know if it wasn't for her excellent care Mom would never had made it through the crisis period. When we were sitting beside Mom's bed, we talked to her. Lee said this was the best thing to do; our voices could be a comfort to her. Eventually, they gave her medication for "induced coma", the doctors didn't want her to wake up, at least, not yet. Two days later, they began to slow the pumping of the ventilator; they had to see what would happen. Miraculously, she began to breathe on her own, her heart rate and blood pressure stayed stable. They decided they would remove the tubes that evening; this would be the deciding factor. The doctors were amazed at what happened, she remained stable, she was breathing on her own. They said it was a miracle, and that her will to live helped her in the battle. Little did they know of the battles she had already fought, and the odds she had overcome.

I told them I had to brush her hair before she woke up, there would be hell to pay if she saw her hair in such a state. Her hair was her crowning glory, no one saw her with a bad "do". She always had such beautiful hair, I guess the pictures attest to this. That was the one thing everyone commented on, AnnaBelle's hair.

I can't describe the relief and happiness we all felt when she finally opened those blue eyes of hers. I could see the confusion etched on her face, but she gave me a weak smile. We weren't allowed to stay long, Lee took over and said rest was in order, for everyone. She told us all to go home, get some sleep. My aunt and one of my many cousins had also spent hours at the hospital keeping a vigil over this woman that was so well loved by all. The rest of her brothers and sisters received regular updates.

Within two days they had moved Mom out of Critical Care, and into regular room. The doctors were still in shock over her rapid recovery, they continued to ask her if she remembered anything. She repeatedly told them "no, nothing". Then during the second day of her recovery she told Kathy and I that she remembered going for the test, and then feeling as though she couldn't breathe. She was in a panic to get back to her room where there was oxygen. Her next words were chilling, she said "I did have this dream, I looked up and the entire headboard of my bed was glowing with light and it was shining through prisms. It was the most beautiful thing I had ever seen, then it seemed as though someone was pulling it away from me. I kept telling them not to take it, I wanted to keep it." We just sat there and stared at her for a moment, then looked at each other. There was nothing to be said. Mom was oblivious as to what had happened, but both Kathy and I knew.

Kathy had told me about the panic in the emergency room when they rushed Mom back to her room. There were doctors and nurses everywhere working on her. They wouldn't let Kathy leave the room, they put her at the head of the bed, leaning over Mom, and told her to keep talking to her, yell if necessary, which she did. She told me Mom was fighting them and thrashing about. Suddenly, Moms arms went limp and her eyes rolled back in her head. Kathy had told me that she knew at that moment, Mom had died. Then the doctor thrust a large needle in her chest and they made Kathy leave the room. The next time she saw Mom, she was on life support.

Now we knew why the doctors were persistent in their questioning about what she remembered. They knew, as did we, what had happened. Neither of us said a word to Mom about what had occurred in the emergency room, this would not have been a good idea. Nor did we comment on the "beautiful prisms" and the light. It could have scared Mom, I know it scared the crap out of me. But then I felt a sense of calm and relief. Now I knew. I knew there was such a thing as "the light". I took great comfort in this news. At the same time, I thanked God for bringing her back to us. She didn't need to know how close she had come to never waking up. However, our secret wouldn't stay a secret, she ended up finding out about her experience.

They released Mom from the hospital three days after she had been released from Critical Care, and the ever watchful eye of Lee. Her recovery was nothing short of the miracle the doctors talked about. I remained in Florida for a few days after Mom returned home, and then flew home. That was the first time Mom ever broke down when I was leaving to go home. The shuttle was waiting to take me to the airport, I gave her a hug and kiss, suddenly she started crying. I could see how hard she tried to hold it in, but she couldn't. It broke my heart, it still does. She kept saying "go, you have to go". I finally left, but as soon as I got through the check points at the Tampa Airport I called her, I just had to hear her voice to make sure she was okay before the plane took off. She said she was better, she sounded better, but it still did nothing to ease my mind.

As soon as Mom arrived home from the hospital , the doctor assigned a nurse to come in daily and monitor Mom's vital signs. She would generally stay about an hour. Again, she questioned her about what had happened, just as her doctor had done.. Did she remember anything? This time, Mom did tell her about this crazy dream she had. Unfortunately, my heart sank when the nurse told her it sounded as though she had an "out of body" experience. I was so afraid it would be upsetting to this woman who had already suffered enough. The effect was quite the opposite, she thought about it for a few minutes and was thrilled with the prospect of what had happened to her. She, herself, began to tell everyone that would listen. To have validation to such a controversial issue was rare, I knew we were blessed.

We spent many good times together over the next few years. During one trip, Mom, Kathy and I went to the St. Petersburg Museum. They had the Princess Diana Exhibition on display at the time and Mom really wanted to see it. We had to find a wheelchair for her, weakness was keeping her from walking distances. But it didn't matter, we had a wonderful time.

On another occasion, we met with our childhood friend, Linda Quimby, now Daniels. We spent the better part of the day at the Municipal Pier, where we had passed so many summer days when we were young. I found I felt as though I had just left her the day before. The forty years in between simply melted away. It's so rare you are blessed to have such a friend, and I have truly been blessed. She is still a treasure to have as a friend. She recently sent me an e-mail, she had bought my first book, and was about half way through reading it. Now, that's a friend.

We celebrated the birth of our first great-granddaughter in September of 2004. Her name is Ashlynn, and she was blessed indeed to be the first great-great-granddaughter of AnnaBelle. And in return, AnnaBelle felt blessed to have her. We now had our five living generations, each firstborn was a daughter. Mom was thrilled. In April of 2005 we all managed to be in Florida at the same time so we could make the photographs that will be treasured forever, those of our five generations of women together. Mom was 78 years old, Ashlynn was 7 months. It was love at first sight for Mom, she loved that little girl so much. We had been lucky enough to have the same situation when I had Jenny. She too was the fifth living generation, and the first granddaughter for AnnaBelle. Sadly, my Grandma, Minnie, passed away shortly after the pictures were taken.

The validation of Mom's experience in Critical Care the first time didn't help much, when less than four years later my beautiful Mother, my cherished AnnaBelle slipped into a coma that she couldn't recover from. All the prayers in the world would not bring her back this time. I tell myself, on a good day, that I had her with me for almost four years longer than I could have. It never helps, but I say it anyway. The tears start again, I cannot let them overflow, quite sure I will never stop crying if I start. "This is not what she would have wanted", falls on deaf ears. "Time heals all wounds", also overrated. Strangely, the one comfort that comes to mind is that she did finally come full circle. She ended up back in her beloved St. Petersburg, and here is where AnnaBelle would have wanted her life on earth to end. If end it must.

I am surrounded by Mom's treasures, all the pink and gold items that adorned her home. AnnaBelle's favorite color was pink, you can be sure that everyone who knew her was aware of this. Her clothes, her jewelry, and her home, all aspects of her life contained as much pink as possible. She found pink furniture where none should have existed. I have part of her pink bedroom set here in her room. It sets ready for her arrival, as though she may walk through the door at any moment, maybe for one of her yearly visits. Even her beloved bedspread with the pink roses covers her bed. Everything is arranged on her pink dresser the same as she had it when she would wake up every morning in her bedroom in Florida. Even her "White Diamonds" sits there waiting for her.

I know these are all just "things". But they give me comfort, I know it's all I will have in this life to care for. As my son, Johnny, so eloquently put it when we were trying to discuss who would get what when his Dad and I are gone; "It's just stuff, it doesn't mean anything. I don't want any of it, I want you here with me". Beautiful words, but an impossible reality.

I sometimes feel that my dreams and my journey with Mom have ended. But then, I know AnnaBelle, they will never end. Just when I feel like giving up, she gives me the little boost I need to continue. Without her strong spirit, this would never happen. But then, without her, none of this would have happened.

I need to go now. The pink dresser needs dusting, the room needs airing, and the pink coverlet on her pink chaise lounge needs the dust shaken from it. I know she sees it all. I know she feels my tears. I know she wants to stop the pain. She knows she cannot.

To Mom

How many ways to count the tears,
     That never cease to flow.
I stay awake, though sleep creeps in,
     I cannot let you go.
You were the one that brought me here.
     Thru years of pain and love.
And now it seems you have to go,
     To someone else above.
I love you so, my dearest Mom
     We've so much left to share.
But life again has left its mark,
     My soul has been stripped bare.
It's hard for me to comprehend,
     What life now holds in store.
I miss our chats, your laugh, your love,
     All this, and so much more.

Carolyn Sue
October 6, 2007

My Beautiful AnnaBelle   2004

AnnaBelle   2004
St. Pete Beach…… Her favorite place to be.

Carolyn Sue   2004
I didn't know until later, Mom took this picture of me.
With Mom at St. Pete Beach, one of my favorite days.

Epilogue

I now feel my work is complete. In all probability this will be my last non-fiction book. I have nothing else to say at this time. (Isn't that funny?) My promise to AnnaBelle has been fulfilled. The first book I published, "The Journey, The Dreams, & AnnaBelle" didn't feel complete to me. I felt she would have wanted more detail. I tried to accomplish this without being too repetitive. Then one day I decided to throw caution to the wind, and just write. I believe there may be people who will enjoy the story without the poetry included. At least, this is my hope.

I still miss Mom more than I can say. I will never be able to face that she is no longer here. Mainly because I know she remains with me daily. She helps me to remember, she helps me to locate previously lost items, she gives me comfort. I have Mom on video during her various visits over the summers she spent with us, I haven't been able to watch them since her passing. There is also a video recording of an interview my cousin taped, she narrates what her life was like growing up. As much as this video would have helped in writing this book, I cannot bring myself to view it. Not yet.

When Mom was admitted to the Palms Of Pasadena Hospital in St. Petersburg for the last time on September 29, 2007, John was in Lutheran Hospital in Ft. Wayne. He was recovering from the first of three kidney surgeries he would have within a four week period. Time was of the essence with these procedures. It was impossible for me to be in both places. No one should ever be faced with such a decision in their life. I thank God for the family I still have. While dealing with loss of my Mother, which was the worst thing I have ever been through in my life, I also dealt with the loss of part of my family. This was the family that I loved so much, and had trusted forever. It has been almost two years, it took most *of that time for me to come to terms with them in my heart. I find great comfort in knowing the one thing that I hope they also realize…. AnnaBelle's Spirit saw it all.*

I flew to St. Pete as soon as I was able to leave John on Wednesday, Mom passed the next morning, Thursday, October 4, 2007. I flew back home on Saturday, John had his second surgery on Monday, October 8, 2007. I know Mom was waiting for me, so I could have that last kiss and touch her one more time. In my heart, I know her spirit left her poor little body the Sunday before. I felt her presence in a sudden rush of air that swirled around and covered me like a soft lacy shawl. I knew she had joined Grandma, Grandpa, and all the others who were waiting for her. Even though my heart broke at that moment, I could feel her freedom.

I will pursue my third book, which I have already started. It is fiction, and shall remain so. With this, I can let my mind run amuck. Yes, I know, it already does. The thoughts of being able to take a plot anywhere I want it to go is exciting. Like a dream takes you in so many directions, to so many places, with so many people.

I'm going to start working on the publication of my children's picture book series too. I have put everything on hold to complete this book, but now it's time to take care of business.

John and I will celebrate our 44th anniversary on August 1st this year. Unbelievable, absolutely unbelievable. I don't so much wonder how, as I always wonder why. He continues to put up with my little quirks (to put it mildly), and I continue to wait, and ask myself daily, as I have for 44 years, what the hell I'm doing here. Then I look at him, and I know. We see what we want to see in the end.

I want to thank you all for your support and words of encouragement. Without it, I doubt I could have completed my work.

Through the pain, the tears, the frustration, and the emptiness of losing the one constant that gave me life, I still have AnnaBelle's Spirit.

Carolyn Sue